# Blac      n

# Afghan

## Rags to Riches to Wealth

# Kevin B Cody

outskirtspress
DENVER, COLORADO

Outskirts Press, Inc.
http://www.outskirtspress.com

ISBN: 978-1-4787-2326-4

Outskirts Press and the "OP" logo are trademarks belonging to Outskirts Press, Inc.

PRINTED IN THE UNITED STATES OF AMERICA

# TABLE OF CONTENTS

# INTRODUCTION

**The year was** 2007, and I had just finished my military career and was happily debt free with thousands of dollars in five different bank accounts. Through my eyes, my future appeared as bright as bright can be. Who needs the military? I thought. I'm good right here. However, in two short years I'd have to eat my words and grovel in the difficult answer to that question, as all the good I had gloated about turned into shambles that I could not pick up. I was twenty-five years old, a divorced father of one, and broke! Not only that but now I was in debt for $20,000 and at a loss for an explanation on how all this happened to me so quickly! Tracking backward a few years to when I was twenty, I had just completed my associate of arts degree with a double concentration in business administration and criminal justice. I had also completed my paralegal certification, and I was in the process of completing my bachelor's in accounting. But no matter how deep I got into the financial aspect of education, I realized that college would not teach me what I wanted to know, and that was the inner workings of finances. When I was growing up, my dad always told me, "Experience is the best teacher." I say that to say this: I wanted to know about money, moola, dinero, and how it works, how to make it, how to manage it. I wanted to know where it comes from, who is at the foundation of it. Why is it that money is so abundant and plentiful everywhere, yet more people are without it than with it? My curiosity preceded me. I had to know, and I would trek on until I found out. That was the education I longed for, be it by experience or the right connections. I was ready, but where could I go to learn? Who and or what could teach me? The answer was simple and harsh at the same time. Little did I know that time, trials, and tribulations would teach me everything I needed to know and what I wanted to know more about.

It is in fact money that makes the world go around; it is more than a figurative statement. Let's take a closer look at it. Everyone is in pursuit of it—that is why we go to school, that is why we go to work, that is why we save it, and that is why we plan and budget it every day. The only people who do not need money are nuns and priests. But, on second thought, a question arises in my mind. How do they afford the property that their cathedrals and convents sit on, which, by the way, is prime real estate? I took the time to really think about this: I've never seen a Catholic church in a storefront. They need some type of finances to back their worldly efforts. So I guess it's safe to say that even nuns and priests don't slip through the cracks. But that's a story for another time. Back to the subject matter at hand, and that is my must-know on money.

The fact of the matter is I needed money in light of my new situation and my lack of it. I needed to know how to make it, and once you make it, what's the best way to preserve it, and so on. I was desperate to know the next step. Now fast-forward to age twenty-six; I have just learned how to do it! I have learned the key to this whole money thing! And guess what? No Columbia College, Georgia Perimeter College, Skagit Valley College, Coastline Community College, Central Texas College, or St. Leo University taught me any of it...and, yes, I went to all of the colleges and universities I named. The funny thing is there were three men who taught me: A black man, a white man, and an Afghan taught me, and none of the three distinguished gentlemen was in the same place. They didn't know each other either. I met each of the three as I moved along through my everyday life.

# 1
# THE NAVY

**It was the** fall of 2002, and I was a freshman in college. It was three weeks into the school year. I was working three jobs: Beyond Petroleum, also known as BP; Family Dollar; and a small comedy club called Uptown Comedy Corner. Of course I had moved out of my parents' house because I felt that I needed space, which might not have been the best move at the time. The economy took a turn for the worse, my hours got cut, and I had rent to pay, so I did what most survivors would do to survive: I joined the military to help myself and to serve my country proudly! From there life took off like an F-18. I was flown off to boot camp from Atlanta to Chicago and from Chicago to San Diego to meet my ship, which would be my home for the next few years. To my surprise, the ship had left San Diego, en route to Hawaii. After spending two weeks in San Diego, I was flown to Hawaii to catch my ship before leaving on what would be the longest deployment ever—all within the first five months of my new military career. However, it all slowed down by the end of the first month on the ship. There was a lot to get used to…the whole shipboard life thing, for one. Sleeping in a small square called a "berthing area," which housed twenty people in what was the size of a closet, was utter misery initially. Each wall in the berthing area had bunk beds, which we called "racks," stacked three beds high. Musty, cranky dudes, overloaded with testosterone, walking around pissed off at life, became the populace I now mingled with, worked with, and lived among. I managed to find privilege in that I could walk outside freely to take in the splendor of the clear night sky loaded with a million stars; the water below me was mysterious and majestic. I now depended on the ship to carry me whole. It was amazing and exciting—at first. But then it got old after seeing the same thing day in, day out. I began to take it for granted, and I wanted a change of scenery. To add to the madness, there were no women within five thousand miles at the least.

I had a plan to save every penny I would earn, since I literally had no expenses. The average person would think that saving money for me, a young guy with no financial baggage, would be the easiest thing to do. But it wasn't quite that easy.

After being on the ocean, circling around for

three months straight, we finally disembarked on the shore of Bahrain, a country I never knew existed. As we slowly pulled into what appeared to be a massive island with oil platforms protruding sporadically throughout the expansive sand, my first reaction was "What in the world did I get myself into? If this is what the world outside of the United States looks like, I don't want to see it." After the ship finally moored to the dock, it was liberty, or what Americans like to call quitting time. I walked off the ship and onto the pier that looked to be a mile long. It was 104 degrees in the shade; I had never been so hot in my life, but at the same time, I'd been on this ship for the past three months of my life, so never mind how hot it was; I was on a mission. I walked to the beginning of the pier where cab drivers awaited our arrival. They held up signs and banners informing us of their service to us for our choosing. Out of all the signs there was one in particular that caught my attention. There were three words sprawled across this sign that were the greatest three words known to man: "Girls, Girls, Girls." I never ran so fast in my life.

"Girls, you want girls?" the cabby said. "Yes, strip club, please take me to the strip club," I said desperately. He looked confused as he replied, "Strip club? What is strip club? No, strip club...girls!"

I was so upset. What could he possibly mean by girls but no strip clubs? What else could he be talking about? Trying to stay calm, I stopped and took a breath. I decided to allow him to show me what he was talking about. If it didn't turn out the way I wanted, I would go back to the ship and sleep my way through this port visit and pray that the next port visit would be an actual country I'd heard of. As we rode off, leaving the pier, the roads became deserted, and sand gusts blew hard across the windshield of the small '88 Toyota Camry that I now rode in. For about the first twenty minutes of the cab ride, sand was all I could see for miles. We began to drive up this huge sand mountain, and after slowly putt-putting our way to the top, I saw skyscrapers—a hidden city was being unveiled right before my eyes in the middle of the desert. The city was just like any US city; the only difference was the men wore turbans, and most of the women were draped in long black gowns covering every inch of their bodies. Every so often you would see an Asian or an African here and there. We stopped at a building that was in excess of twenty stories high. The cab driver had a smile from ear to ear. "Here we are, girls!" I walked in, and there was a man standing at the front desk. I was thinking to myself, there must be a lounge somewhere in here, but there wasn't. There wasn't even a bar. I was pissed off.

"Where are the girls, man? You said girls!" I griped.
…..He replied evenly agitated. "Yes, girls!"
"What in the world, dude? You lied," I complained.
"Come, come, let me show you," he finally offered.
…..We walked into an elevator and went up to

the fifth floor. The doors opened onto a long hallway with doors along both sides and a set of double doors at the end of the stretch. We passed all the side doors and continued straight to those double doors. He opened the doors, and I peeked in to see two Asian females in a king-sized bed engaged in enormously explicit acts that dropped my mouth to the floor. The cab driver laughed so hard he could barely stand straight up. When I finally snapped back to reality, I considered the fact that the building we were in had to have at least thirty floors, so I asked to see another floor. We proceeded to the sixth floor, and there were Russian women in every room. On the seventh floor, there were Malaysian women, and on the eighth floor, Filipinos. On the ninth floor was the be-all to end-all. I saw something I'd never seen in my life and have yet to see at any adult entertainment night club that I've ever been to (and trust me when I say I've been to quite a few in my day). The wow factor was her nationality. As an American I'd been forced to see these people as malnourished, potbellied beings moping about with fruit flies flying around and landing in their eyes. They could do nothing about it. They always had dirty feet from walking barefoot throughout their daily routine. Yes, that was by way of US television depictions. But in this room on the ninth floor was a woman who was the epitome of beauty. She was Ethiopian, and, need-less to say, that's where I stayed the whole time I was there and seven times after. She stayed on the ninth floor, second door on the left. I don't remember what number, but I knew exactly where to go whenever my ship pulled into that port. I was nineteen and in love. I even tried to get her pregnant on purpose just so I could bring her back to the states. But, of course, that was a far-fetched dream because she was, in fact, a prostitute to my dismay. In retrospect I am ashamed of that fact as I was sincere in my desire to make her my own. Any man would have done what I did if they'd just seen her! Any man would have paid for it.

The lesson was hard and could have cost me my health. At age nineteen, new to the world, I was naïve to the core, thus my behavior. What I learned was that these women left their countries to do exactly that— prostitute! They made great money and sent it back home to their families so they could have what was needed to raise kids, live, eat, and keep a roof over their heads. It's a shocking trade-off, but that is life for those beautiful women, and they know what they are doing; they are handling "business." I've been frowned upon for my participation, but lesson learned, and I'm still alive and healthy, thank God.

All in all, that's pretty much how the year over-seas on the other half of the world went. Whether in Thailand, Singapore, Bahrain, or Dubai, drinking and sex and more drinking and sex was my lot. Indeed it was what it was, and if it took my money, so be it.

At last the long, tedious deployment was over. It was late November, we were just making it back home to port in San Diego. The guys were excited and eager to see their wives and girlfriends. They could finally manifest some plans and desires, such as going on that trip they were saving all their deployment for and/or purchasing that new car or even do an add-on to their house. This made me think as I walked off the ship to explore downtown San Diego. I stopped at the ATM to check my money, and my balance read $430.32 in checking and zero in saving. I hadn't saved a penny, literally. Other shipmates of mine had saved tens of thousands of dollars, and I had nothing to show for my eight months overseas. I had made, at the least, twenty-five thousand dollars and had nothing to show for it. I was as broke as a joke.

San Diego, California, was beautiful and always sunny. It might have sprinkled maybe once the whole year and a half I was there. I recall sitting at Oceanside, a beach in San Diego, where there was always a Lamborghini parked along the strip or a drop-top Bentley with some young guy perhaps a few years older than me sitting behind the wheel. What did they do, they weren't rappers? How was it that they could afford these $250,000-plus cars? I thought to myself, I need a plan. I needed a way to make some money aside from my military paycheck. The only thing I could think to do as a sidebar was to go into sales. Either I was going to sell drugs or CDs. Now, as for drug sales, that couldn't possibly go over well since I was a military; everyone knows where that road ends.

Besides I wasn't built for that lifestyle, and I couldn't fight. As for selling CDs...what would I sell? I couldn't sing; however, I could write songs, and I could rap just a tad bit.

The thing about rapping is if you can't rap, you can always have a nice beat with a tight bass line and chant some motivational chants, and every so often throw a nigga or two in there, and there we have it, a hit!

I met this guy on the ship whose name was Boyd. Everyone either called him "T Boyd" or, more appropriately, "Mean Mug" because his face was grimaced and crumpled up all the time, as if anger had painted his face fresh and new every morning. His look really did suit the nickname. He was a beast, and he listened to no one unless he felt like it, military officer or not! He hailed from Houston, Texas, and represented Texas to the fullest, speaking about his state fondly. As mean as he was, he managed to say good things about Texas and his growing up there as well as his schoolmates, too. In fact he spoke about a well-known rapper that he went to school with who went by the name "Lil Flip" and how he could rap better than he did. He was, in fact, the best freestyle artist I had heard at the time. He was interested in the idea of making a mix tape, so he teamed up with me to make one. We began going to a studio named Bat Cave, which happened to be owned by one of Nick Cannon's close childhood friends.

I discovered some habits of studio dwellers, such as I'd become, which were kind of comical. One period of time we were all in a studio with a producer called Drew; it was around the same time that Kanye West had just dropped his debut album. Perfect timing for us because it became motivational music for us, and our creativity flowed even better. Most artists or rappers always appeared to be on the tipsy side of life. They seemed to need, perhaps prefer, to smoke marijuana before, during, and after a session to enhance stimulation during their recording time at the studio. Well, being in the military and never having done drugs in my life, I found satisfaction in drinking a forty-ounce. It was the only stimulus I needed.

Yes, I was still only nineteen at the time, which meant I was an under-age drinker, but who cared? I was in the same flow as everyone else as I sat in the lobby of the studio under the influence, while T Boyd was in the booth recording his verses. The front door of the studio swung open, and low and behold Nick Cannon himself came through the door. He was real chill and respectful. He had just released a movie entitled *Love Don't Cost a Thing*, which was actually pretty good. When he came through the door, he held it open until a sexy, short, light-skinned woman walked in. She had on a short plaid skirt, and her hair was black, silky, and crinkly. She was a sexy female indeed! On a scale of one to ten, she was a definite ten!

Nick and this woman walked into the switch-board room where Nick began to talk to his friend who owned the studio, and that's when I heard the music stop. Very shortly afterward T Boyd and Drew came out of the studio, walked through the lobby, and out the front door. I got up to walk outside behind them only to find Drew talking on his cell phone to a friend excitedly. "Dude, you won't believe who's at the studio right now!" he raved. I couldn't believe it.

Why would he be on the phone ranting about Nick Cannon being in the studio? I thought. Not that Mr. Cannon isn't impressive in every way, but... After a brief pause, Drew finally replied, "No, Christina Milian. I am not joking, dude; she's like right in there right now with Nick Cannon!"

Wow, Christina Milian, live and in color, glow-ing majestically right in front of our eyes. But then I realized Nick Cannon's new movie had costarred Christina, so it stood to reason why they might have been there together. My jaw dropped as I overheard all this, especially the part about Christina, but then I looked to my left and saw an unusual looking SUV. I'd seen Cadillac Escalades, Tahoes, and Expeditions, but I'd never seen this SUV. It looked way too flashy with peanut butter plush leather seats, and a cream color exterior. From the looks of it, I knew it had to be pretty pricey. Nick was somewhat of a paid man. So of course I didn't think he would ride in anything less than $100k. The front of this ride read Range Rover...

sexiest SUV I'd ever seen indeed. Once again I saw a successful man other than me.

That was my motivation. I completed the mix CD and began selling them like my life depended on it. After the first week of going out after work, I made fifty dollars; after the second week, another fifty dollars; the third week, fifty dollars; the fourth week, zero; and the next three weeks after that, zero. I made a whopping $150 off my hard work and dedication, but I had spent $3,500 all together on the production of the product. I learned a big lesson about overhead and production cost. First of all, before I go into an investment, I needed to do my research to figure out exactly how much it would cost to make the product or the investment readily available to potential customers. Then I had to create my break-even analysis, because anyone who invests is going to want to know how much he/she needs to sell to recoup the money they invested in making the product, and secondly they can find out exactly at what point he/she will actually start seeing a profit. Then I had to decide whether it would be a short-term investment or long-term investment and prepare for the worst.

Now let's revisit my mistake with this whole mix CD thing. I spent $3,500 on overhead and/or production cost. I would have had to sell seven hundred CDs at five dollars just to break even, hence the phrase "break-even analysis." Needless to say, I didn't sell that many, and I didn't sell them for five dollars. I got desperate after the ninth person told me at Mission Beach, "You're a nobody. Why should I pay five dollars for your CD?" So I said, "Fine, buy it for three dollars, and if you think it sucks, I'll refund your money. That worked a few times but not enough to make my money back. The first investment on my way to success was a disaster, and it ran me straight into the ground.

My job title on the ship was deck seaman. When you first get in the navy, you have to work your way out of the deck department, which is the bottom of the barrel. I worked my way out of the deck department and into the ship's office where I worked as a legal man, which is what the navy calls a paralegal. I applied for this job in the military, and it didn't quite work out. Because of the contract that I signed, I could either be a legal man or master at arms. A master at arms in civilian terms is a law enforcement officer. Since I didn't get the job as a paralegal, I had to apply for the law enforcement job, so I did and I got it. I weighed the pros and cons. Going on deployment on another ship was not a favorable option; I would just waste my money. Instead I figured if I was stationed somewhere, in one place, I could create a good financial routine, start saving and investing, and possibly even settle down and get married.

As it turned out, I did just that: I went to the navy's Law Enforcement Academy, and while I was there, I got married to Shuntae, not necessarily a high school sweetheart but a sweetheart I just happened to have met while in high school. She was eighteen and I was twenty. We had been dating for about three or four years, and one day we eloped in San Antonio, Texas.

After graduating from the academy, I was stationed in my birth state of Washington. My duty station was on this little island two hours from everything—two hours from downtown Seattle, two hours from Vancouver—but I can say the nearest mall was only forty-five minutes away, so I guess that was a plus. Whidbey Island was my new space, and I'd gotten to know it well. There were four small towns on the is-land, but I resided in the town of Oak Harbor. When I first got there, I secured a nice place on the top of a hill that overlooked the sound and the mountains. Anyone who has gone to Washington knows that the average day is misty and cloudy, but every so often it's actually sunny; and on a day when it's sunny, the sky-line of the mountain ranges takes your breath away. After I'd done all the paperwork and the place was officially mine, I furnished it and bought my wife a ticket to Washington so we could start our new life together. I also asked my friend Nathan to join us in Washington because it would give him a chance to start a new life as well.

Nate and I had been friends since the summer of 1995. He and his family moved from Stone Mountain, Georgia, to Nashville, Tennessee, in 2000, which meant trouble for Nate. Trouble found him, and he courted it quite a bit. By 2004 he was in over his head, and I felt for him. So I figured that if he moved to a whole new state and had a solid foundation, he could focus, handle his business, and get ahead in life. Shuntae, Nate, and I got settled in, and everyone already knew this would be a good opportunity for all of us, and this was time to take advantage of it.

My plan was to start saving as much as possible and get out of debt, start school, and complete my degree. However, for starters, the move put me $4,000 further in debt. To add to the madness, I decided that I needed a car, so I got the first car I could get my hands on: a used 2002 Hyundai Elantra with fifteen thousand miles on it for $15,000. No more than a week later I was watching a commercial that advertised a brand-new 2004 Hyundai Elantra for $9,999. That really sucked; I kicked myself a million times for my premature, stupid decision! My decisions were beginning to cost me greatly, and the grand total was now up to $40,000 worth of debt. Enough already, it was time to finally be the successful man that I was destined to be. But of course the inevitable happened.

It was four months into my new life, new marriage, new military career, and a new beginning…and the military called me to deploy. It was 0500 and I was ordered to be in Chief's office by 0600. I reported at 0545. When I walked in, Chief's exact words were "Take this week off; you will be going on deployment for temporary duty next week. Here are your orders."

"Roger that, Chief. Permission to carry on." "Carry on."

I walked out of Chief's office pissed, scared, and excited, all at once. I didn't know what to say. I didn't know what to do. My mind was ripping with thoughts and options. Shuntae and I had just gotten adjusted to our new lifestyle. Nate had just started a new job and college. I couldn't just pull his feet out from under him. At the same time, if I put the apartment up, and Nate went back to Nashville and Shuntae went back to Georgia, I would be able to save an extra $1,000 a month. I nursed those thoughts for a while, but then I had to really consider what was most important and most fair. I decided I would keep the apartment and give both Shuntae and Nate one bill apiece. I would go on deployment, save what I could, and pay off as many debts as possible.

# 2
# DEPLOYMENT

**I deployed, and** it didn't take me long after I got there to dub it the anus of the earth as it was the worst deployment ever. Nonetheless, I'm glad I went because it taught me a great deal. Yes, it was there where I decided that active-duty military was not for me and would probably never be. It was there that I realized that in the military I wasn't a person; I was a number and not an individual. I was a number to be used and abused at the government's discretion. But of course for every major decision there had to be a turning point that solidified a major decision; mine was a pep talk from the army general over the base at that time. His exact words were:

"I would like to thank the men and women of our armed forces for the blood, sweat, and hard work that is put out on a daily basis, but we must understand that we are in a time of war. We are going to have some casualties, one of us or some of us will die, and we're going to have to suck it up and continue the job that was passed down to us with great honor, courage, and commitment."

Everything that was said so far in this general's speech was OK. I was cool with the fact that there was a possibility that one of us would die. There are, in fact, casualties in war. But what was said thereafter was what made me stop and rethink this whole situation.

"But we will not let not one detainee die."

"What?" I felt like that was the most insane pep talk I had ever heard in my life. The fact of the matter was whatever politically correct name they'd created for these individuals that we couldn't have die, we would have to just suck it up? That fact alone that I could die and the enemy's life was protected was bull crap in itself. At that point it wasn't about the military; it was about me, about my life, my family, my money. I really began to think things through. I had a son on the way, and it was an absolute must that I get out of the military. Before you can actually understand my frustration and anger, one must understand the conditions. It was hot. I literally stepped outside dry and within ten minutes or less, because of the humidity, I was drenched in sweat, as if I had jogged a mile or two. Not only was the climate unbearable, but the job sucked; I manned blocks six days a week, sixteen hours a day. I don't care what anyone says, "Them is slave hours, boss."

During my deployment I had the opportunity to talk with two distinguished gentlemen; one in particular really made me think. I was in a room with two men, but I had to stay in this room for forty-eight hours straight without falling asleep. For a second I thought that I was forgotten and left to starve with these two guys. I was not to talk to these guys at all, and I didn't for the first sixteen hours. But after so much laggard time, I went crazy! There are only but so many mind games a man can play with himself, having absolutely nothing to do. One of them spoke silently in a raspy voice, "MP." Since he didn't call me "nigger slave" or "nigger," it kind of caught me off guard. I tried to keep a strong, stoic face because I wasn't going to allow him to break me. Besides, if I talked to him, I would be in trouble, major trouble. I held up until about the twenty-seventh hour. I was tired and hungry and, hell, just plain bored. He asked, "MP, you are free; do you feel free?" I looked at him and replied, "Yes, I do." He then said, "Look around, MP. You are in the same cell as I. You have to follow stricter rules than I. You can go but only so far; can you come and go as you please? Can you fly home and do as you wish? No, therefore you are not free; you are like me, MP. You are a detainee." Dang! I hated to say it, but this dude was absolutely right. We began to carry on this conversation some more, and his counterpart began to look at him with disgust, as if talking to me made him a traitor.

Somehow our conversation led to the subject of finances and economics. He said, "Americans...stupid Americans. You don't believe in the principles of finance; you only believe in credit. See, my people know of no such thing. We have capital or we have nothing. We have land, crop, cattle, or we have nothing. There is no credit." So I asked him, "How do you buy a home for your family? How do you purchase a car? How do you buy clothes?" He chuckled. "Stupid American." By now I was thinking to myself, since I'm so stupid, why are you in here? But, for the record, those words never came out of my mouth.

But he was absolutely right. I didn't know the difference between a want and a necessity in life. In my thoughts about these truths, I came to the conclusion that I had to immediately begin to cut back on a lot of things that were not necessities. It made me think of all the wants I got by being stupid with my checks. At the same time, this conversation pushed me to begin to think differently and begin to get out of debt. I came to the realization that getting out of debt was not a want, it was a need; and as long as I owed anyone, I would never completely have full control of my life, and I would never be completely free. One who owns all of his belongings and owes no one owns his life.

# 3

# HOME SWEET HOME

**The deployment had** finally come to an end, and the mental brutality that I took during this short span of time will forever be burned in my brain. The best part of the experience was I did walk away better than when I went in. During my stay, to better myself and keep my sanity in Guantanamo Bay, I managed to pay off a lot of my debts and put money away in a retirement fund for government employees called the TSP (Thrift Savings Plan), and I completed a great deal of college courses.

We landed in Jacksonville, Florida, and it was only a matter of time before I would see my wife, who was waiting in Washington for my arrival. I hadn't seen her in just about a year, and she was due in weeks. I left a newlywed husband with a new military career and was returning a changed husband and a soon-to-be father. I had accomplished so much in a short time span, and I was going to accomplish so much more not being secluded and limited to what I could do. Now there are no limits. My wife and I could begin building our future.

I got home, and Nate and Shuntae weren't even speaking. I hugged my wife, and of course the first thing on my mind was to go straight home to give her the business. Nate was still at work, so we took advantage of that whole block of time before he came home. I told Shuntae we had to talk about a few things regarding our living arrangements. We were lying in the bed, holding each other, and I told her that I had decided to get out of the military, although I might stay in the reserves, but I knew for sure that I was getting out. Before I got out, it was an absolute must that we get completely out of debt. We both had at the least an associate's degree and a few thousand saved. She agreed with me on me getting out and the goals that I had planned for us. I had two years left, so we had to get to work ASAP.

Nate came home later that night, I gave him a hug, and we had a few beers. I asked him how school was, and he told me he wasn't going this quarter, but he would start back next quarter. "Oh, you're not in school? That's messed up, Nate!" I told him. I explained to him that I hadn't put up the apartment because of school just for him. What completely angered me was when I found out that he stopped going to school a little less then a month after I left. I don't think he realized what he had done to me, and what I done for him. I was livid. All I could do was walk away from the conversation.

The next day I pulled up my credit because I needed to know where Shuntae and I stood financially and found that we had at that time a little over $17,000 left in debts. As I scrolled through, I found that the satellite bill was in collections and the Verizon phone bill was in collections, too. Hmm…these were the two bills that Nate and Shuntae were to pay while I was gone. I decided to check and see if the phone was on, but there was no dial tone or anything. Then I turned on the TV and nothing. This couldn't be right; it really couldn't be. There had to be some kind of mistake. They both worked; they both had modest incomes. I paid rent, the car note, car insurance, and utilities, which only left them the TV and phone bill, and of course food. So why and/or how did these two bills go into collection? Seriously, this was a huge problem.

By the time Nate got off work the next day, I was still a little heated about him dropping out of school, but I switched subjects and immediately questioned him about the phone bill. "I didn't have any money. I'll pay you back," he said. "Where is your money going, bro?" I asked him. He replied, "Man, I have to pay Rent-A-Center for my bedroom set." Now I knew full well that bill was maybe $200 a month. He still had a nice chunk left over. "OK, well how much did you save?" I asked. "I know you got a few hundred in there, dude. Just pay the collection off, dude; it's only $239, bro." He couldn't because he had not saved anything.

What I didn't understand was the fact that he worked all kinds of hours, lived completely free, and had literally next to no bills at all, yet had nothing to show for it but a bedroom set that he was renting to own—and even with that he was barely keeping up with those payments! The first words that came out of Shuntae's mouth was "I told him to pay it." I turned and looked at her and instantly "Shut the F up!" flew out of my mouth. I never thought I would say such a thing to my wife whom I loved dearly, but I continued hammering away now at her, too. "What bill did you pay? Why wasn't a little eighty-nine-dollar satellite bill paid? Why is that off, too?" I fumed. "You mean to tell me you make twelve hundred dollars after taxes a month and you couldn't pay eighty-nine dollars? Where in the world did your money go? Whatcha been doin'? We don't even have a kid yet, and you already broke! I know you ain't saved nothing 'cause I seen your bank account, so what are you talking about?!"

I stormed out of the house and slammed the door. I had to go somewhere, anywhere but in that house with the two of them, so I went to the city beach to clear my head. I realized that I had a mess on my hands, but it could be cleaned up. Hey, I'm smart and

I have drive and lots of motivation and energy. I can definitely take care of this, I thought. I mean really it was only about $300 worth of debt…I could take care of that with my next check. I had to pay off Shuntae's debts along with mine anyway. In fact I had to get the whole "yours and mine" attitude out my head…we were married.

Soon I came up with an idea. I knew a few comedians from when I worked at Uptown Comedy Corner, but my brother Kenny Wayne knew them better than I did. Since I knew that I could get ahold of comedians through my brother, I decided to do a comedy show. I chose Bremerton for the location of the show because my grandpa owned a restaurant, lounge, and bar called the Hickory House. The only issue that I might run into with doing anything at the Hickory House was family. My family in Bremerton was no joke—not all of them, but there's a few uncles who like to hop in the middle of things when they see something great but don't like to get in at the beginning and do all the hard work. That was neither here nor there, so I proceeded with the show.

A comedian by the name of K-Dubb agreed to do the show. At the time he was a pretty well-rounded comedian and was about to really take off. He had a stunning resume that boasted connections and work with the likes of Bill Bellamy's *Who's Got Jokes*, Jamie Foxx's *Laffapalooza*, P. Diddy's *Bad Boys of Comedy*, NBC's *Last Comic Standing*, and BET's *Comic View*.

He was featured on Field Mob's sophomore album, *Ashy to Classy*, to name a few, as well as a plethora of other things and things to come. He is truly an underground king of comedy and funnier than most comedians I've ever heard or enjoyed.

My brother and I spent $1,500 on the show. The expenses included liquor, plane tickets, hotel room, flyers, a few props here and there, and a DJ—and there you have it, my first comedy show.

I pulled in good $1,200 at the door and $3,000 from liquor sells. It was the greatest feeling of accomplishment to know that something that was on my mind could be brought to life. It put me on this high that topped a forty-ounce any day. I can't even explain it. Doing this deal taught me something about the way that bars and clubs work.

We purchased three cases of liquor. When you have a liquor license, you have to purchase liquor in cases. Liquor could only be purchased by the fifth or more, and there are twelve fifths in each case; each fifth only cost seven to nine dollars apiece because each bottle was at wholesale. There were only about sixty people who showed up that spent on average fifty dollars apiece on alcohol and the twenty-dollar entry fee. We made $4,200 in four weeks, from a $1,500 investment. That's practically 200 percent interest in one month. What CD or mutual fund does that? None of them! After the show was over, my brother and I were counting the money. We had eight stacks of

$500 on the table. There were a few cousins around the table, as well as an uncle and an aunt standing over us like vultures. My uncle began talking to Kenny Wayne about how he helped with the show, and if it weren't for him, the show would've been nothing. What happened was my uncle asked my brother if he could get up for a few minutes before K Dubb and tell a few jokes, my brother agreed. So my uncle got up for about ten minutes and made the crowd laugh. That was not hard to admit. The guy is funny. The problem was that my uncle was saying that we owed him money for his services. Neither Kenny Wayne nor I said we would pay him, but he insisted that we pay him for his ten minutes. My brother wasn't having it, but I'm more passive. I figured we should give him fifty bucks, what the hell! But Kenny Wayne stood solid on not giving him a dime because he didn't state that he would get up and tell jokes for money; he asked specifically if he could get up and tell jokes for a few minutes. Money wasn't a part of the conversation. The funny thing is a week into the promotion for the show, I had asked a cousin and other friends of the family if they wanted to invest in the show or help with promotion itself, and everyone was busy; no one wanted to help or invest. Now money had been made, and of course everyone felt that they deserved a part of the profits. Why? I have no idea.

Kenny Wayne started taking the money and stuffing it in his pockets and demanded, "Hey, Kevin, grab the leftover liquor, put it in the car, and take K Dubb back to the hotel." Kenny Wayne had the most serious, pissed-off face I'd ever seen.

I returned to the bar after dropping K Dubb off at the hotel. As I pulled up, Shuntae was standing outside of the bar and waving at me to hurry. I got out of the car and heard glass bottles shattering and chairs and tables falling. I ran in to find my brother and Uncle Kenny having a full-out brawl. Kenny Wayne is a big, black, muscular, 230-pound, six foot three ugly gorilla. My uncle weighs about 170 pounds and is five foot four. Needless to say, Kenny Wayne was pounding him religiously. I ran to try and break up this fight. I guess my Aunt Lidya thought that I was trying to help my brother beat up my uncle. First of all, Kenny Wayne didn't need any help with this situation; secondly I had more respect for my uncle than to use any type of physical retaliation toward him. I also prefer to communicate effectively in other ways about money issues. Besides, I can't fight anyway.

While trying to break up the fight, my Aunt Lydia jumped on my back yelling, "Get off my brother, get off my brother!" I was outdone! I could barely breathe with this woman on my back, but I said to her, "Aunty, I'm trying to break it up. Chill, Aunty!"

I finally got Kenny Wayne to get off my uncle and got him in the car. I told Aunt Lydia I would come back next weekend, and that I was sorry. I dropped Kenny Wayne off at the hotel, and I left to go back up to Whidbey Island; of course I was in the military and had to be at work at 0545, and it was 0145. From Bremerton to Whidbey Island was a four-hour drive, so this would be a night that I didn't sleep. I could make it because my take-home was $2,250 and Kenny Wayne's was $1,950. That sounded really good and looked really good until running the numbers. I found after running the number that it wasn't right and actually negotiated myself into getting the shorter end of the stick, which I didn't realize until a few days later.

Let's go a little deeper in the mathematics of the promotion. I invested $900 in the comedy show, and Kenny Wayne invested $600. So I asked myself why it was that I only made $300 more than he did. Looking at the numbers, I pretty much did a little more than double my investment; I turned $900 into $2,250 when everything was all said and done. Kenny Wayne turned $600 into $1,950, which is a little over 300 percent interest or, better put, he tripled his investment. It doesn't take a financial guru to understand that I screwed myself in this equation. For a while I felt that my own brother screwed me over, but I couldn't necessarily say that, because during the negotiation process, we were talking about our returns from the investment. Remember, I wanted it to be simple and painless. However, when you are dealing with short-tempered people, painlessness is questionable. Regardless I knew Kenny Wayne had the money, and he was a risk-taker like me, but he was not a good person to work with as far as business was concerned. So I told him I would put in $900 but would need $600 and we'd split the profits fifty-fifty. To my surprise he agreed in no time, with no complaints or gripes. I should've known to really look into the reason why he would actually agree without putting up his own argument, but whatever. My dad always said experience is the best teacher, and this mind-boggling experience taught me the key to a little something called "profit split."

I now know that it is only fair when an investor's profit split percentage is equal to the percentage of that investor's contribution toward the overhead. For example, the show cost $1,500. I invested $900, which was 60 percent of the overhead, and Kenny Wayne invested $600, which was 40 percent of the overhead, so the correct and fair profit split would've been sixty-forty. Meaning I should've gone home with $2,520, and Kenny Wayne should have gone home with $1,680. I t was a successful event, unsuccessful negotiations. But I've learned from this mistake, and I will never make moving forward.

# 4

# GETTING INTO THE MONEY

---

**A new year** arrived and with it my newborn son, which meant that I was laden with a few new realities, one being that this new small life, whom I loved more than anything, was now dependent on me for absolutely everything. This new emergence in my life found me holding near and dear to three specific people I called real friends: Shuntae, Jamie, and Nate. I considered Jamie to be my little big brother, and Nate was simply my brother, hence my son's name. Yes, I named him after all of the people I loved, Keshun Aaron Alexander Cody. Of course I couldn't resist adding a little ghetto ingredient, like combining Shuntae's name with mine to create Keshun, but from there I made sure the rest of the name was somewhat respectful: Aaron is Nate's middle name, and Alexander is Jamie's middle name.

A few months into this new year I had adjusted to life as Daddy and was enjoying my time with my chunky baby, who was now dropping dumps like a man. Changing those full diapers was not pleasant, but that was my baby and I loved him. I often held the little man while he slept as it was my joy to do so. One night when he was asleep in my arms, I thought to myself, I have a year and a half left in the military, and I have a few classes under my belt but no degree. What am I going to do? Since there is no way I'm staying in, I need to do something to ensure that my finances are in shape. The first thing I did that night was pray and ask for forgiveness for my wrongdoings, made my confessions, and asked for wisdom.

The next day I ventured out to the library in hopes of finding something that would help me. But what would I look for and in what category? I went to the finance section because I knew I needed to educate myself in that area of my life, and after some perusing, a small blue and black book entitled *Money Mastery* caught my attention. I gripped it eagerly and opened it up to the first chapter, which was entitled "Money Is Emotional." I sat down and read every word of the first chapter and found it to be profoundly true, not because I could compare the information to anything I already knew but because it just made sense to me and seemed to be the beginning of an answer that I could actually apply to my life immediately. That first chapter alone taught me that if I control my emotions, I can and will control my finances.

People spend money emotionally every day. Sometimes people spend money to keep up with the Joneses, and some people spend because it makes them feel better; the money they spend is all emotional money. It's an easy concept, but it's not easy to do because, if it was that simple, everyone would be well off.

Another thing I learned from this book was the most important method of all. It was called the Power Down Method. This can and will help anyone in debt, and it will allow indebted people to knock out their debts in no time, as well as help keep the person in debt motivated to do better. Most people would say that when you're paying off debt, you should start with the debt that carries the highest interest rate. Well, that sounds good, but let's really think about this. If there's a $5,000 debt with 30 percent interest and there are about twenty debts to pay, it will take almost a year and a half to pay that one debt off. And tell me, how will someone feel after paying off only one debt out of twenty in a year and a half? They will most likely feel like they haven't progressed at all. So the book suggests that paying your debts off from the smallest to largest debt would be the best bet.

Before starting on the smallest debt, what has to be figured out is how much money can actually be contributed to debts out of your monthly income. After finding that number, divide that number by the amount of debts, which in this case is twenty, and begin paying them off one by one. When the smallest debt has been paid, take the money contributed to the debt that was just paid and add it to the next smallest debt; therefore debts get paid faster, and seeing debts actually starting to diminish will keep the motivation to continue doing the same thing. Here's an example:

| Amount allotted for debts $100/5 = $20 | | | | | | | | | | | | |
|---|---|---|---|---|---|---|---|---|---|---|---|---|
| Debts | Allotted Each Month | | | | | | | | | | | |
| Phone = $30 | $20 | $10 | $0 | $0 | $0 | $0 | $0 | $0 | $0 | $0 | $0 | $0 |
| Speeding Ticket = $70 | $20 | $30 | $20 | $0 | $0 | $0 | $0 | $0 | $0 | $0 | $0 | $0 |
| Doctor Bill = $120 | $20 | $20 | $40 | $40 | $0 | $0 | $0 | $0 | $0 | $0 | $0 | $0 |
| Credit Card = $350 | $20 | $20 | $20 | $40 | $80 | $80 | $80 | $10 | $0 | $0 | $0 | $0 |
| Loan = $ 500 | $20 | $20 | $20 | $20 | $20 | $20 | $20 | $90 | $100 | $100 | $70 | $0 |
| Total | $100 | $100 | $100 | $100 | $100 | $100 | $100 | $100 | $100 | $100 | $100 | $100 |

After I finished reading that book, I was hungry to learn more about finance. I wanted to learn how to invest in the stock market. I didn't want to read any of the so-called "for dummies" books, but I did find another interesting book entitled *24 Essential Lessons for Investment Success* by an investment guru named William O'Neil. The crux of this book was investment.

It not only showed me how to build a solid foundation to stand on as I learned investing but also motivated me and encouraged me to open a broker account so I could dive into this world with some success. I opened TD Ameritrade account and began purchasing penny stocks.

I bought penny stocks called LOUD, CRAY, and LAMP and made $100 here, $200 there. It became an emotional roller-coaster ride from day to day. I worked like this: I bought LOUD at sixty-four cents and sold at sixty-seven cents. Then I bought the same stock again the next day at sixty-nine cents to try and make another $300 in literally minutes. But it dropped down to sixty-six cents, and my emotions got the best of me; I took a $300 beating, and that was how my day-trading life went for the next three months.

One day I was looking for stocks that were super cheap like around ten cents or lower, and I found numbers I didn't know existed. I found stocks for .0016 and .0024! These stocks really sparked my interest since they were less than a penny. These I could definitely afford! I continued looking and found a stock worth jumping on. I believe it was ILGY at a mere .0004, and I purchased 175,000 shares of it on a Friday. I purchased on Friday because usually everybody is getting off the market for the weekend, and that's when the stocks drop.

Monday morning I woke up at four o'clock as I always did to catch the market when it first opened.

When I'm on the West Coast, I make myself a cup of coffee and log onto my Ameritrade account. Well, on this particular morning, I was sitting at my computer after turning it on, sort of waiting for it to come on completely. When my Ameritrade screen came up, I logged in, and that is when the hot coffee dropped on the floor and began soaking into the carpet. "Oh, my God! Oh, my God!" I hollered with my stare wide and frozen on the screen in front of me. I reached over and Shuntae was peacefully sleeping on the right side of the bed, but still I began tapping her vigorously though my face was still glued to the computer screen. Unfortunately, I didn't realize that I was not tapping a shoulder but was instead slapping her face a million times a minute. She woke up pissed and slapped the crap out of the back of my head. "Kevin, what's wrong with you?" she yelled. I was so in shock I didn't even feel the pain from the slap. I grabbed her face and said, "Look at the screen, baby, just look at the screen." She asked, "What am I looking at?"

"Look at the bottom left, Shuntae." She looked and asked in a calm sleepy voice, "Is that how much we got?" I nodded slowly with a slight grin on my face and happily answered, "Yes." In no time she had made it to her feet and was jumping on the bed and then made her rounds through the house, too. That was a happy woman that day. The next thing I did was grab the phone and call my dad to tell him what I had done. When I told him I had made a lot of money in the stock market, he didn't believe me. Fine, I thought, and I asked him if he was in front of his computer. He was, so I gave him the log on and password to my Ameritrade account. My dad is a pastor, so of course his first question was "How much is 10 percent of that?" The next thing I knew, the phone lost our connection.

This stock that I purchased at .0004 Friday had opened on Monday at eighty-one cents, and I had purchased 175,000 shares of the stock for seventy dollars. That turned a profit of $141,750. How much interest was that? I got carried away with thoughts of the type of Bentley I was going to buy. I was temporarily caught away but was brutally brought back to earth with a glimpse of the clock. The time was 0704, and I was supposed to be at work at 0545—and I didn't care like I might have a week prior because on this day there was $141,750 in MY account. I didn't have a worry in the world.

As obligation would have it, I went to work and meandered into the police department with a smile on my face. Chief was pissed. I wanted to kiss him. He was a short, stocky white guy with a mild case of small-man syndrome, and he was fuming. His face was as red as Rudolph's nose, and he looked hotter than two squirrels humping in a wool sock. "MA3—in my office! Now!" he spat. "Moving, Chief," I responded.

I was standing in his office at attention in front of his desk, with a smile permanently engraved on my face. I was high on life and felt as if I was floating, and no one could bring me down. Chief asked as calm as he possibly could, "Cody, why the fuck are you late?"

"Permission to speak freely, Chief."

"Speak, Cody."

"Chief, relax just a little. Chief, I think you might need a hug. Chief, come here. Chief," I said, standing with my arms opened wide.

"Do I look like I joke around? Do I look like I'm joking with you right now? How about I send you to joke with the ole man," the chief threatened.

Usually when navy personnel speak of the "ole man," they're referring to the captain of the base or the ship. In most cases you go through this process called "captain's mass" where the individual in trouble receives his/her punishment, which is in the form of a loss of rank or money, or just restriction. At this point I made more in one week than this guy would make in the next three years or so. By this time I was thinking to myself, he can blow me. My reply was "Chief, do you really want to know why I was late? I can't tell you but please just allow me to show you." I asked Chief if I could use his computer. I pulled up my account and showed him the six-digit number on the screen. "What's this?" he asked.

"That's how much I just made off some stock I purchased for seventy dollars last week; I was celebrating with my wife this morning and lost track of time." His mouth dropped to the floor as he looked at the screen.

He sat there for no shorter than twelve minutes, literally. Eventually I quietly walked out of his office and shut the door and proceeded to the watch commander's office, my direct supervisor, to see where he wanted me. He said, "MA3, grab your unit, man. Hurry up. You're zone twelve."

For the first time ever, I had a crap load of money, but I soon learned the difficult part about the stock market, and that was deciding whether or not to let it run with the opportunity of making more profit or to keep the profits I'd made…that $141,750. The money was there, the opportunity was there, and so were many, many emotions. I didn't know what to do. It was the hardest decision I ever had to make because at this point I'd no longer be investing, I'd be gambling. So be it, I chose to roll with the punches and keep the money flowing.

As I watched throughout the week, the stock was up and down. I watched my account go from $141,750 on Monday to $120,000 Tuesday; it opened at $135,000 on Wednesday but closed at $87,000. I wanted to hold for one more day to try and get out at $100k at the least, but it didn't quite happen that way and dropped down to $42,000. OK, that's where I decided to draw the line, but the problem was when I tried to sell the stock it wouldn't sell. The volume didn't support it. For example, if a stock volume is at $1 million and you have a hundred thousand shares, it would be easy to sell the shares because the volume is there. But in my case I had 175,000 shares, and the volume was at $20,000 for the whole day. I could only sell $2,500 worth, which was good for nothing. On Friday the volume was at $15,000, and I only sold one thousand shares, and pretty much for about a week or so, I was slowly selling the remaining shares. By the time all the shares were sold, I made about $36,000, which sucked but was still pretty good considering the fact that I invested seventy dollars.

I continued to invest in various stocks and fluttered throughout the weeks. Even so, I religiously searched for that next big high-risk stock, but I never found it. The good thing that came out of it was that I was able to eliminate some debts; I paid off Verizon, Dish Network, Freedom Electronics, CitiGroup, and a crap ton of other small debts between $500 and $1,500. For the first time in a long time, I was finally at the point where I only had about $15,000 worth of debt that included a credit card, a loan, and a used Hyundai Elantra that I purchased ignorantly for $15,000 with thirty-five thousand miles on it, when a new Hyundai Elantra at the time with zero miles on it cost $10,000.

# 5

# THE BREAKUP

**Personal debt was** consistently fading behind me, I was two classes away from my AA, I had completed my paralegal certification program, and each bank account had at least a few thousand dollars in it, leaving me feeling like I was diversified enough. I was convinced life was headed in the right direction for sure, but I felt Shuntae and I needed to be planted financially whether or not I left the military and found a job. What if I didn't find one right away? Regardless, I knew I had to know where we stood right away, especially now that I had one year left to serve. Expenses by this time had also been cut down to practically nothing, due to war. There's nothing like agreement between two married people, so I was glad she agreed with me until I told her what I had in mind:

I told her we should move out of our luxurious

apartment and into the smallest, cheapest trailer that we could find. It was a great idea, I thought. At the time she was making $1,200 after taxes, and I was raking in $2,300 after taxes, so my rationale was that we could put away my whole monthly income and live off hers without suffering much. We could still go out to eat every so often as well as do some of our favorite things, such as going to Vancouver to party, because she was still under age at that time. Well, she turned down the idea real fast because she felt as if we would be taking steps backward. I argued that we'd be taking steps forward, but I understood why she would feel that way. She grew up in the same area of Atlanta as a well-known rapper who goes by the name Gucci Mane: zone six off Bouldercrest and Flatshoals Road. She lived in a three-bedroom, one-bath home that housed her sister and her, her two uncles, her mother, her grandmother, and two aunties. I could imagine her not wanting to live that lifestyle again because she had gone from the hood to Hollywood in a sense. However, my point was totally missed for fear that we'd live like trailer trash for the rest of our lives. Not my intention at all. This was a temporary plan; all I wanted us to do was cut back for a short time frame, save money, invest money, and then we could live luxurious for a lifetime. By no means did she like the idea, so I gave her the opportunity for input. I asked, "What do you think we should do?"

"I DON'T KNOW!" she replied.

After some thinking and sighing, I resigned to the fact that perhaps living in a one-bedroom trailer with a newborn could be kind of harsh. So I came up with another idea: house sharing. A married friend of mine whom I worked with in the military had just purchased a home and was looking for a roommate to help him and his wife pay the mortgage, so I suggested to Shuntae that we should room with them. We looked into it and found that they were offering $500 to stay with them, utilities included, with a fifty-fifty split for the cost of food. Brown and I worked at the same place, so we could car pool to work every day and save on gas. This situation would allow us to save and invest about $3,000 a month. It was actually better than the first idea, so I asked her what she thought about it. Again I received a resounding, "I DON'T KNOW!" which pissed me off beyond belief, but I swallowed my anger and took a deep breath. Just then another idea popped in my head, an angry emotional idea that could actually work. I presented it to her with all the frustration it deserved, and it might have come out like this: "OK, how about this? You go back home to Georgia since you're not saving or doing anything with your money anyway, nor are in school for that matter. Go down there and find a job and get settled in before I get down there. That way, when I get out of the military and come home, you will already be situated. I'll continue school and stacking up my money up here and finish paying off the rest of my debts, because being stupid I paid off all yours first, and I will do my shows and keep investing my money up here by my damn self."

"Hell no, Kevin, so you can be with those little hoes that be hanging around after the shows?"

"OK, so what do you suggest?"

"I DON'T KNOW!" she said. That was it. I was done and stormed off. At that point I couldn't talk to her anymore, not another word. I slammed the door and began walking down to the beach. As I walked, I thought to myself, Kevin, what's wrong with you, man? You fell in love with an airhead; that's exactly what you did, you dumb piece of shit. Why? Pops told you, man, he told you and you didn't listen. You spoiled her, that's what you did. You just can't stop tricking, can you? [Tricking is when you spend money on a girl who's offering you a dream.] I swear you have just as much brains as she does—none at all!

Of course I didn't tell her these things because I would never put anyone down like that, especially while being as angry as I was. That is also why I walked out, because when I'm angry, I can say and think and do some harsh things.

This stressful argument with my wife led me to begin hustling harder than I ever had before, because now I really had to pick up her slack and keep my drive and motivation at the same time. So I was doing comedy shows in Oak Harbor and investing in the stock market. I remained in school, and before long I was only months away from finishing my degree while working twelve-hour shifts, fifteen days a month with the military. Of course that left no time for Shuntae and me. Right before going to sleep, I would spend a little bit of time playing with my son, and many times I would fall asleep with him and wake up the next morning and do it all over again.

My police precinct shift was from 1800 to 0600, which translates into 6:00 p.m. to 6:00 a.m. in non-military time. We worked a three-two-two-three schedule, which meant I would work three days, be off two days, then work two days, and be off three days. It worked itself out to where I would be off every other weekend.

At work there were usually two officers to a unit, which meant most of the time I had a partner. On one cold windy work night, my partner and I were patrolling as we normally did. We were doing our normal vehicle patrol in Whidbey Apartments on a Friday night around 0330 a.m. because that's when a lot of the sailors were returning from the clubs and house parties; there was usually one or two house parties going on. I was in the passenger seat of the unit; my partner was driving and he asked me, "Hey, Cody, why did you park down here at Whidbey Apartments, bro?"

"What are you talking about?" I asked him. "I didn't—" I stopped in mid-sentence as I looked up to see my car sitting outside of this apartment building, thinking this can't be. I know she wouldn't. I am a good man, I work extra hard, I hustle my butt off for my family, and I know this is not how she would return the favor. I looked at the license plate that read 695 NYA, proof that it was in fact my car sitting at 0330 in front of someone else's house. How could it be? Shuntae didn't have any female friends, so whom could she be "visiting"? Hopefully, for her sake and mine, she has some girl friend I just never met. I said to my partner, "My wife probably came to one of her friend's house to get drunk or something. It's cool, bro; let's go." We left, and when I returned home that morning, I didn't say a word about it. Saturday night was the same thing as well as Sunday night. I said nothing. On Monday and Tuesday I was off, but Wednesday and Thursday night the same thing.

By the time Thursday rolled back around, I was sure it was a dude she'd been visiting, and I was pissed. Not good, especially since I had a 9mm with a fifteen-round magazine in it and two fifteen-round magazines in my magazine holder, plus a whole gun belt full of toys and gadgets to use on the both of them. And to think this girl was bringing my son out of the house in the middle of the night to this guy's house, and when I got home every morning, she was stretching and yawning, "Good morning, baby!" as if she was excited to see me, knowing she'd been getting dick inside and out the whole night before. The thought infuriated me. I think I know myself fairly well and consider myself secure and confident, so why would I hate on this guy who's banging my wife when I'm on an island full of women who would love the opportunity to bang me? I guess I was the stupid one for actually staying faithful the whole time. I was right about my self-assessment. I was an airhead.

I spied and played dumb for about four more weeks, and sure enough the same routine continued with her. No problem, because during that time I was setting up my living arrangements to move out of the apartment. By the fifth week, I put in a two weeks' notice with the landlord and told her that I would not be renewing the lease. I also made storage arrangements with my friend Nate for the furniture. He freely allowed me to store them in his available space.

The whole time Shuntae had no clue that I knew about her affair or that we had to be out by the end of the month, and by this time it was the last Sunday of the month, and we had to be out on Monday! Well, I arrived home from work at 0630, and Shuntae performed her normal routine, stretched and yawned as if she'd been home all night and couldn't wait for the moment that I walked in the door. When I did, she jumped on me, saying, "Baby, I missed you! Good morning!" and kissed me with her arms wrapped tightly around me. Amazing, seeing as how this dude gave her the business last night. How did he do that? He needed to give me some pointers!

"What's up, babe?"

"What do you want for breakfast?"

"Hold on, babe, I will be right back. I forgot something at the precinct."

I left and came back with two buddies, Nate and Bill, along with a U-Haul truck. Shuntae was in the kitchen cooking breakfast when I walked in the house. Nate and Bill walked in behind me to her shock and dismay. "Come here," I said to her as she looked at me questionably. "We need to talk real quick." I escorted her to our room and closed the door. I began, "Baby, we have to be out of here today, so that guy whose house you've been at every night that I'm not home for the last few months—the one who lives at 904 in Whidbey Apartments—I need you to ask him if you could stay with him. No worries, babe. I'm not mad, really. I completely understand, no hard feelings; it's cool. We don't need to argue or nothing; it's truly OK. What's done is done. I still love you, I promise. So just call him and tell him you need somewhere to stay. I mean I'm pretty sure he won't mind at all." She stood there for like twenty minutes, speechless. She looked as if she didn't know whether to start crying or start screaming. While she stood there dumbfounded, I walked out of our room and signaled for Nate and Bill to begin helping me move the furniture into the U-Haul truck. She called this Tim guy, and he came to pick her up. When he came through the door, I gave him a nod, and I pointed at him, "You got it, bro."

I had no hard feelings toward him; he was just a

squirrel trying to get a nut, and Shuntae was not an ugly female. I had no emotion, no anger, no sadness, or anything as she hopped in his Titan with our son. As they drove off, I felt a huge weight lift off my shoulders; it was like the world had no limits. I guess the pain and the hurt was somewhere within, but it never came out. Perhaps it became the fuel that boosted negative energy into motivation.

Life went on. I completed my degree the following month, and the shows were raking in $3,000 to $5,000 on any given night. After too long it was definitely time for me to move on to bigger and better things, but before I could do that, I had to set myself up to do so. In my foresight I saw one tremendous show that would yield upward of $20,000 that I could pocket. My wheels began to turn, and my imagination delivered a perfectly masterful idea that was sure to be a money-maker: Comedy Show Promotions.

# 6

# THE BIG ONE

**Yes, I was** the mastermind behind the whole promotion thing, but unfortunately I had limited myself to producing one show every four to six weeks in Oak Harbor only. It didn't take long to realize that I had to fix that or I'd end up sabotaging my own success, so I decided to cover the whole Puget Sound area, which included Washington's most popular cities and towns such as Bremerton, Seattle, Oak Harbor, Tacoma, Everett, Auburn, and of course the capital, Olympia. I'd planned to take the Puget Sound by storm. The idea was to do a tour of Washington's seven hottest cities, which inspired the name "Puget Sound Comedy Shutdown." It was a seven-city tour that would last a whole week, from November 1 through 7, and would be comprised of small shows and venues. This educated me on how to increase the streams of revenue.

The first stream was the cover charge collected at the door; the second stream was in the menu items, like alcoholic beverages and/or finger foods. At the beginning those were the only two streams I could think of until going out to other events. My eyes were opened to a ton of new streams of revenue, for example, the door money from the after-party, parking, other menu items, pictures, autographed T-shirts, and even advertisement slots on the flyers, posters, and other paraphernalia good for advertising. In all, the overhead cost that was most expensive was not labor but the venue itself. I thought to myself, if I could put myself in a situation where I didn't have to pay for the venue, I could cut my overhead cost down a great deal...at the least 20 to 30 percent.

I planned out a way to make this happen beginning with a things-to-do list. The first thing I needed to do was sell the show or the idea and the venues. The second was to sell the show and the venues to the entertainer. Third and lastly I finalized my marketing strategy.

After my list was completed, I started plowing away at it and put a proposal together. I wrote down ten possible bars, nightclubs, and other venues in each city. After pinpointing the venues that I wanted, I began cold-calling each venue, trying to set up meet and greets to present my proposal. I locked in all seven venues, which turned out to be a major milestone that I conquered. Now it was time for the second phase; it was time to present the venues and ideas to the entertainers. It took all of four hours, so there it was—done. We had the venues and the entertainers, all the parts needed for the show to take off.

Once I got rolling, it took exactly five months to set up the whole tour—the entertainment, flights, hotels, and venues. Everything was locked in and ready to go. Once the tour was set up, I decided to take a weeklong vacation to celebrate. During this week my brother Derrick, who had just graduated from high school, came from Atlanta to visit me, and I wanted to show him a good time, especially since I had not seen him in four years. On that Thursday night, I took him to a club in Tacoma called The Factory, and it was definitely poppin' for a Thursday night in Tacoma. I let him use my ID to get in since he was only eighteen at the time. We were privileged to be VIPs with access to a few drinks and women to mingle with and flirt with. I took a second to look around and thought to myself, I need to find out who the promoter of this event is. I wonder if it's possible for him to help me promote my events.

I started asking around until finally the bartender gave me the name Echo. What a charge went through me at the sound of that name. I was finally getting somewhere, and I could feel it. Soon I was running around the club asking strangers if they knew Echo. Everyone knew her but couldn't point her out. But finally a model-looking chick at the front of the club did point her out to me, and I was thrilled. When I turned around to see the infamous Echo, I beheld the sexiest pair of legs ever. My eyes followed those legs down to the pair of four-inch red stilettos she was wearing. My eyes then rolled back up to her perfect body in a skin-fitted red dress that introduced me to every curve of her body—her small waist, beautiful tits, and nice round ass that tooted out the back just enough. To top it off, she had the most gorgeous smile I had ever enjoyed; she had the whitest pair of straight teeth imaginable. It blew me away. She sashayed past me and headed up some stairs toward the VIP section. She seemed a bit bossy or, maybe I should say, in control, so even the bouncer got out of her way. That side of her appealed to me even more.

Curious and fearless, I followed her to the VIP area, took my stance, and fixed my gaze on her because I knew that once we engaged in conversation, I'd have to conduct myself in a strictly business manner. But until then all I could see was that she was the epitome of sexy, and I wanted to pounce. After a few minutes, I had to shake myself out of the horny toad mode and into business mode. Even though I was pretty drunk by now, I pulled myself together enough to make my approach. Extending my hand slowly, I tapped her on her slender shoulder. She turned around and looked me dead in the face. She looked even better up close, and she smelled so good. "Hi, I'm Kevin Cody. Are you Echo?"

"Yes, that's me," she responded.

"Listen, I like the way you got this place really packed. I need your assistance in helping me with a little tour I put together. Do you have a card or something? I'm kind of messed up right now and don't wanna talk business with you with alcohol in my system." She gave me her card, I shook her hand, and off I went.

I went off to look for my brother, admiring all the beautiful women on the way. At last I spotted him at a table talking to two hood rats. I was baffled. Why in the world would that be his choice among the smorgasbord of classy, good-looking women all around us? There were Pilipino, Malaysian, Brazilian, Ethiopian, and sophisticated black women and Swedish women everywhere, yet he still found the two most ghetto women in the place. My guess would be, since he just came up from Atlanta, that's what he was accustomed to and he got in where he fit in.

It was around 0230 and the clubs in Washington close pretty early compared to hot Atlanta clubs. It was time to wrap up the night and find a little something to go home or to the hotel with. Derrick and I huddled to come up with the game plan. I said, "Check it out, man. I got the two white females on the couch ready to go, bro, so let's get them and go to the hotel, bro."

"Nah, man. Come on, Kevin, look at those two. Look, you get the short one with the big booty—I know you like big booties—and I'll get the tall one," he said, trying to convince me.

"Derrick, broaden your horizons, man. Stop going with what you know…try something different on for size, man!"

"Kevin, come on, I haven't seen you in like three years, man. This is my first time kicking in it with my older brother. Man, come on, man!"

Something told me to stick to my guns on this one, but I didn't. We were out that night for him, so we went home with the two hood rats. My brother told them to follow us, but his girl insisted that he ride with her. Of course her friend hopped in the car with me. I didn't know her name and didn't wanna know; I really just wanted to get the night over with. "Ooh, leather seats, I like the way leather feels against my body," she said while rubbing her ghetto booty on my seats. "Does the heat work? It's kind of nippy." I turned on the heat and the seat warmers. "Ooh, my ass is getting hot." I was thinking to myself, why can't she just shut up and enjoy the ride? I swear I will never let Derrick have his way again. She wasn't a bad-looking chic; she just didn't have any intellect, which for me was an immediate turnoff. We finally made it to Derrick's girl's place after a long, irritating ride. To my surprise we were driving onto a military installation. Aw, man, I was thinking, I hope this isn't one of those military wives that cheats on her husband when they're on deployment. The first thing Derrick's girl said as soon as we walked into her townhouse was "Wait, let me check on my son." I looked at Derrick as if he were crazy. You can't be serious! I thought. Shaking my head, I mouthed to him, "We beat and we're out, ASAP!" We continued on to the living room. There was no babysitter; this girl actually had left her child, who couldn't have been but five to eight months old, home alone so she could party and drink. I saw her pictures in the living room of her in uniform, so I was a little happy that she wasn't married, but she was in fact the military member. We proceeded on to the living room where she popped in a movie and offered us a seat on a couch that looked like it had been passed down from generation to generation. I enjoyed a small moment of pride in my brother as I looked over to see that he had landed a piece of tail the first night of hanging out with his older brother. My pride was short lived, however, because I felt that he could have done a lot better for himself. Humph, it was only one night, and this night would be completely erased from my memory the next morning; so let's get on with it, I figured.

I initiated sex with a little foreplay and such. My brother got the memo and began to indulge his girl, too. Now that both women had been prepped, it was time to beat it down and bounce, but before anything could happen, my girl's phone rang. It was her babysitter telling her that she had an emergency and had to leave, so my girl needed to get home within the next fifteen minutes or she'd leave her kids there. She left in a flash like I guess any good mother would, so I was left sitting there with a hard-on, and my little brother was making out with this chick. Then to my frustration she took him by the hand and walked him upstairs. At that point I texted the white girls, "Let's meet up." They texted back, "Let's try for tomorrow." Now I was angry and through my BlackBerry on the ground. He better not get some, and I don't. A few seconds later I heard bath water. What in the world were they doing? I wondered. Shortly after that my little brother came downstairs with a smile on his face and walked straight to the kitchen, I'm guessing to get something for her. Since he was meandering around like I wasn't there, I grabbed him by the hand on his way back to her, pulled him to me, and whispered, "Hey, man, you better share!"

"Man, Kevin; come on, man!"

"Look, if we went with those girls we were supposed to go with, this wouldn't have happened! You better ask if I could beat it, too."

"Man, dang! All right!"

He walked his ass back upstairs to relay my desire just as he should have, as far as I was concerned. I heard their muffled voices talking back and forth through the closed bathroom door and running water. After words were exchanged, I heard, "What! Hell no!" "Baby…" he begged.

"Get outta my face! Get out my house!" she hollered, pushing him along as they both walked down the stairs draped in nothing but towels. She left him downstairs and went on about her business fuming.

Derrick came and plopped down next to me on the worn sofa. He was truly angry, and I didn't care. "See, now we both ain't getting none!" Even though I was still very upset, I looked over at him and calmly said, "Derrick, she didn't kick you out of the house; she kicked you to downstairs. She is going to come back down in about five minutes to get you, and you guys are going to have sex for the rest of the night while I sit down here and listen to the both of you all night. I swear I'm never listening to you again." No sooner had I finished my sentence than she walked downstairs, grabbed Derrick's hand, and pulled him off the couch. She turned and rolled her eyes at me. Then, as they walked up the steps together, my brother had the nerve to smile at me while giving me the finger. Sure enough, I stayed on that dirty couch and listened to them for the rest of the night.

The next day I managed to set up a sit-down meeting with Echo at a nice location in downtown Tacoma called Indochine, an Asian dining lounge. For the first two minutes, I heard absolutely nothing she said. All I saw were sexy lips moving, beautiful eyes, sexy thighs, and long, silky black hair. I was completely mesmerized by her beauty and intellect. It took me a while to realize that she was asking me a question. "Huh?" I finally grunted as I snapped back into reality. She repeated, "Exactly how long have you been doing comedy shows?" I started from the beginning and told her all the sordid details of my little road to success thus far. We then began to discuss what part she would play in the comedy tour. I concluded that she had more pull, had a lot more connections, and was more known in the community. I felt that she should take the three major cities, Tacoma, Seattle, and Olympia. We both agreed that $1,250 for her services would be suitable for her load. It was probably the best $1,250 I ever spent. Each location had a different setup and environment. It was like the environments of the tour venues went from one extreme to the other. Everett was a retro metro area; all the cultures collided to make one being. Olympia was filled with well-to-do young adults and older adults who were more on the conservative side. In Bremerton there were meth heads everywhere, but it was a small town where the social classes had a strong cohesiveness, in which case we were limited to marketing to the social class and lower class only. In Auburn the main attraction was the Mulkashoot Casino. For sure we couldn't compete with that unless of course we had the help of the best bar in Auburn by the name of Spunky Monkey Oak Harbor was a small military town where, of course, the military got paid on the first and the fifteenth, so that's exactly where we'd planned for the tour to begin on the first of November. Tacoma was what I considered the hood in Washington; it consisted of the largest African American presence in the state.

It was November 1, the first day of the tour, and I was excited. There were about twenty-five hundred seats to be filled throughout the tour at fifteen dollars a pop, so I was looking at making $37,500. When it was all said and done, my overhead for the tour was about $15,000. Having meetings at some of the best restaurants, such as Oceanaires, Cutters, and Sky City Café, really took a toll, I realized once I added it all up. That's quite a few dollars to spend when trying to wine and dine your way into a deal or agreement.

Going in I felt comfortable; after all, this is would be the place that would go down in my history as the place that molded me as a promoter. I felt as if it would be the easiest and quickest $2,700 I ever made. I didn't spend too much time promoting in this town because it was small, and I just knew all I had to do was send out an e-mail and flyer to a few key locations and my name alone would bring patrons. This night turned out to be the worst of all the nights. Literally a handful of people showed up. I didn't even make a fraction of the $2,700 I planned to make. I pulled in $120, and that was only because the patrons who did show up gave donations based on how entertaining the show was. I was surprised that the comedians actually went ahead and performed for the eight customers and seven employees working that night. I guess the show wasn't bad at all, just the turn out.

The next night we were in Bremerton at E&J Reyes Casino. It was all right compared to Oak Harbor; we cleared $800, far better than $120. Bremerton lifted my spirits and gave me hope for the rest of the tour. The following night we were in Everett. It was hot, and we had a packed house although we did let half of the seats in the place go for free. I have to admit that if it weren't for the six-dollar steak meals, no one would've come. I do know the owner of Foxy's Steak and Spirits really knows how to promote and advertise for an event, especially with big competition right across the street. In Everett we cleared $2,000. Things were looking up, but after three cities I was still nowhere near breaking even. Going into the fourth show, I began feeling a little more confident; we were in Auburn at a small bar, the Spunky Monkey. It was also a nice packed house, but it was the smallest of all the venues, too. It wasn't packed enough as I only made $500 that night. We gave out a lot of free tickets at this location as well in order to stir up some buzz in the town about us. When I woke up the following morning, I received a call from the owner of Aristocrats, the venue in Seattle. The owner informed me about a few legal complications and that the show had to be canceled. I was supposed to be in Seattle the following night and Olympialast. This news shocked me, and now I began to really stress. Echo and her company took care of Seattle, Tacoma, and Olympia, and all three cities had been buzzed about us and were expecting us. Tacoma and Seattle had the biggest. Tacoma was pretty good to me, as I pulled in $1,500 that night. Better than what I'd been getting. I had no complaints; I was completely fine with that, thanks to Echo and her squad.

The following morning we didn't have a show, and the last venue was in Olympia. I had planned to go ahead and drive out to Olympia and get settled into the hotel for that night before the show. However, my headliner received an exciting phone call and as a result took off for California to try out for a small role in a movie and got the part! My tour was now over! Because I understand that business is business and money talks, I had no choice but to let him go. He had a choice to make, so what was I supposed to do? What power did I have over that? Well, now I could either continue this one last show in Olympia or fold. That night there might have only been a handful of people to perform in front of. So for the headliner it was either do the movie role or perform for a handful of people. Hollywood sounded better than an audience of a few folks.

I called the owner of the Vault in Olympia to see how many tickets were sold, and there were less than a hundred. The situation as it stood was painted like this: I was one comedian short of a comedy show. To find a comedian at the last minute would cost anywhere between $200 and $300. But it was not really worth investing another dime into an investment that had already cost me $15,000. By canceling the show in Olympia, it would tarnish my reputation with the owner and the city of Olympia forever. With all of this in mind, I decided to pull the plug and cut my losses. I swallowed $10,000 and what followed was the beginning of a very dark period in my life.

# 7
# MY GREAT DEPRESSION

**The tour was** finally over, and for that I was truly happy. I could not deny that it had been quite a ride and an exciting journey. I took a few days and sat in my house with my son to reflect on the past few months and pinpoint where I went wrong. I thought I was being smart; I thought I budgeted well, but my budget only included the normal costs. Costs like travel expenses, advertising expenses, and labor expenses were left out. Not to mention the usual overhead expenses like gasoline. I must have used twelve hundred gallons of fuel traveling from city to city. I also didn't include the cost of hotels. There were quite a few times I had to stay at a hotel for a night because meetings lasted longer than expected and I was way too tired to drive three to four hours back home. Let's not forget the cost of all the coffees, mochas, and lattes I drank as well as breakfast, lunch, and dinner. Although I didn't have a job, I still had monthly expenses such as day care, rent, car insurance, and other living expenses. In the process of setting up the tour, I never saw these important and costly factors; I didn't take them into consideration. I was twenty-four and had worked my butt off for absolutely nothing. My thoughts about myself were now damning: I felt that I was always going to be nothing; I was a failure; my marriage was a failure; my business was a failure, too. Anything and everything that I'd do in life was going to fail.

At one point during the beginning stages of setting up the tour, I sat down with an Edward Jones financial adviser in Oak Harbor. I wanted to take a bundle of money and make it move fast. So I went to him for advice. He looked down on me as if I was a nobody, and I was. I didn't have millions like most of his clients. I only had a few thousands. I told him I wanted to make five thousand grow as fast as possible. He asked if I was in the military, and I told him no. I got out because I wanted to put all my time and energy into my business. He asked why I couldn't do the military and my business at the same time. I told him I couldn't because I didn't want to and because I couldn't manage a business while I was in Iraq or Afghanistan or on a ship for that matter. He looked me square in the eye and said you're going to fail and your business is going to fail and everything you do is going to fail. Turns out a few months later he was absolutely right. Besides he said he wasn't in the business of doing quick flips. He invested long term.

This time in my life was nearing the end of 2007, and my son and I were at his mother's house. I drove up to Anacortes on New Year's Eve because Shaunte wanted to go out and party for the new year. Besides I wasn't doing anything anyway, so I didn't mind. What better way to spend the New Year than with family, and Keshaun was my family. At the stroke of midnight, New Year's fireworks went off all over the small town of Anacortes. Keshaun slept right through it all. When the fireworks ended, I realized they symbolized my life. It was a short-lived extravagant show, a bright future. But in the end, that's all it was, a show. No happily ever after.

The middle of January rolled around, and I hadn't seen my parents and siblings in a little over a year so I decided it was time to go home; maybe I wouldn't be as depressed as I'd been. The very next day my son and I were on the first flight to Atlanta. Of course his mother didn't mind. It was her opportunity to be free and do all the partying she wanted.

When I got to Atlanta, I quickly saw that it was a good move and a needed change in atmosphere. The first few weeks in Atlanta I sat around at my dad's house doing nothing. I hung out with old friends here and there, but for the most part, my son and I hung out together. My mom and dad were separated at the time, and often my mother and I would go to the Waffle House to talk. On one occasion, my mother looked very concerned and asked why I looked so depressed. "I'm a twenty-four-year-old with a failed marriage and a failed business, and I'm not even in school," I told her. "I'm not where I wanted to be by this time. I was so far ahead, and now I'm flat on my back." She shook her head like she couldn't understand my reason for saying what I'd said. She responded, "Kevin, it's OK. It's OK to fail. But you haven't failed, Kevin. You have to understand that if you shoot for the stars and you land on the moon, you're still OK." She made me smile, and I felt a little better. I guess in a way I did have my sights pretty high. I guess everyone who loved me felt my depression because Nate called me later that evening. He wanted to know what was wrong as well. He said, "Kevin, if you think you're a failure, kill yourself." You know what? He's right, I said to myself. He said, "Kevin, I don't know anybody else in your position who has done the things you've done at your age. Think about it, man, when you first wanted to do a comedy show in Oak Harbor, nobody wanted to let you do it in their establishment, so what did you do? You rented out a location and did it anyway. That night you shut the whole town down.

"Then what happened? All the bars began calling you to do shows for them, not only in Oak Harbor, but in Bellingham, Burlington, and Everett. You were only twenty-two, bro, on top of that. Look at what you have, man. You have a beautiful son, a two-year degree, a paralegal certification, and the last time I seen your bank accounts, you weren't exactly broke. I only seen two, and both of them had more than $13,000 in them. OK, so you failed at one tour. First of all, you did a tour. How many people you know put together a tour, let alone have the money to finance a whole tour without a job? Man, you don't work!" I sat there silently for a minute. My head was swirling with all that he had just taught me, along with everything my mother had told me. They both were right. I had more money than the average twenty-four-year-old, and I was completely debt free, no bills other than a cell phone bill. In all my accounts combined, I was sitting at around $41,000 and change. Maybe since I was just coming out of a depression, that was not something I should've realized. Yes, I lost $10,000, but I still had money. I had worked so hard with my head focused and tuned in to what I was doing, I never really paid much attention to my accounts. I knew the money was there for anything that I desired, but in a way I wasn't aware of exactly how much. Realizing my financial status couldn't have been any worse than me losing the $10,000. I almost immediately started to do something that we young individuals like to call "ball out of control." Atlanta by no means was Washington. In Washington there were mainly things going on only during the weekend, but not Atlanta; every day and every night of the week there was something to do.

I usually went out by myself; rarely would I hang out with a group of people. During one of my lone outings, I'd gone to downtown Atlanta to a place called The Underground. It was a Tuesday night, and I was at the bar drinking by my lonesome although there were maybe three other people at the bar with me. One guy I knew from the military; other than that the place was pretty much empty. Personally, I prefer a bar with a sparse crowd versus a bar full of people. At some point three women walked in, looked around the club, and turned to leave. Obviously they didn't see but the few of us at the bar, so there was no reason to stay, I guess. But I got up and chased them. "Whoa, where are you guys going? You just got here." One of the women replied, "There's nobody here; I'm not about to waste my time." I replied, "There's nobody here because you're about to leave. Have a few drinks; it's on me. Let's go." What group of women is going to turn that down? They followed me back into the bar at which time I told the bartender that whatever they drank was on me for the rest of the night. My BlackBerry went off, and it was a text from a female I'd met a few weeks prior. It read, "What are you doing?" I replied, "Drinking by myself, U?" Her answer was "Nothing, bored." I said, "Come downtown to The Underground and hang out with me for a while." She replied, "OK." About a minute later, she texted and said, "My sister's coming, too." Then a few minutes later she said, "Her sister's friend is coming, too." I texted her, "It's cool; just get down here." The night began looking up. It was going to be a replay of my younger adult years of partying, drinking, and sex. Lots of sex.

When the three women walked in the door, my eyes were fixed and I was all but salivating; I could not stop gawking. Maybe it was the double shot of Patrón straight I'd just thrown down my throat, or maybe they were just the finest three women I'd ever seen. Most of the time there's an ugly one and two cute ones, or even two ugly ones and one cute, or plain all out ugly. But in this case they were all dimes. Jasmine was in the middle as they walked into the bar and came straight to me. I was struck dumb. When they sat at the bar, I didn't know what they wanted, so I ordered for them blue MFs—five rounds. After the last round, we were all wasted. Even the designated driver couldn't drive, so we were going to have to get a hotel for the night or stay with my friend Lavender who had an apartment not far from The Underground. I called him and he complied. Jasmine, her two girls, my friend Lavender, his two friends, and I all piled into this little apartment. Lavender and Jasmine's sister weren't drunk like everybody else, so they just chilled while everybody tried to sober up. Jasmine's friend was passed out in the chair with her legs gaped open with a dress on. She was wasted for sure. Jasmine was on the floor passed out but half coherent. The crazier thing was that one of Lavender's lady friends was digging Jasmine's friend (the dark-skinned one). Might I add here that even though she was a girl, she was a bit butchy looking. Jasmine's friend was so tore down that she didn't even realize the butch girl was pushing up on her and making her way up her dress at which time she proceeded to take her pleasure with her. From there the night was long, crazy, and oversexed.

My life remained in this vein for a few months. I wasn't progressing at all. I looked at myself and realized that I was turning into someone who would never do anything concrete in life. I started to get a strong sense that I was truly better than where I had landed, and that was in a place of doing and accomplishing absolutely nothing at all. I felt that it was time to return to the land that made me who I was. I was ready to return to show business, the life of the hustle and bustle, so my son and I caught the next flight we could find back to Washington.

Once I got there, the foundation was set; I had multiple investment accounts like TD Ameritrade, Forex, and Edward Jones. I set my finances in place to sustain growth. Also, after making the move to Washington, I begin looking for a location to begin promotions while setting myself in line to start where I'd left off, but the inevitable happened. It was November 2008 when I woke up to find that the market had taken a turn for the worse. During this month it turned out that I lost more than 35 percent in my two mutual funds, so I did what the average person would after seeing a huge drop: I sold the shares and took the loss. I traded the American dollar against the euro and lost 75 percent in my Forex account in one trade. I suppose this is why we follow the market and the market doesn't follow us. Although, in our everyday lives, we influence the fluctuation of the price of stocks and bonds, inflation, and everything else that has something to do with the financial markets in an inevitable relationship.

I fell right back to the bottom of the bucket. But this time I was really at the bottom. I'd lost the only thing that I felt, at the time, could help me get back to being me; it was the crux of who I was, and now I had lost the money that took me years to build all in one day. I was sick to my stomach, and all I knew to do now was to retreat, shy of becoming a recluse. The more time I had to myself to think about what transpired, the more angry I became toward people—not just anyone but people who controlled certain aspects of life, like those who dealt with our finances. These people get paid to make choices, good and bad ones. Apparently mostly bad choices and they get paid regardless! Of course the people that I speak of are brokers and so-called asset managers. They're the smartest, dumbest people in the world, and yes, I said "smartest, dumbest." They're smart because they get paid to lose people's money, and they're smart enough to choose not to get paid from what they produce but smart enough to get paid a percentage of the overall amount. They're dumb because they mostly lose people's money and don't have the decency to feel just a little remorseful for what they have done; it is like they are callous and blind to the pain and agony they cause families on a constant basis. But what bothers me the most about the way the whole financial investment arena works is the way that they go about handling the structure between the investor and broker/manager; they've made it so that the only one who takes the risk is the investor. They can define it that way, but the truth is the "risk" is truly "robbery" and needs to be recognized as such. To think that this is perfectly legal is sickening.

After a while I felt Washington wasn't working out, so I did what I do best: run. I ran from my problems and thought I could just start all over. But the drawback with running is the problems you're trying to leave behind never get resolved; therefore they are still with you. I learned at twenty-four that the only way to really defeat or solve a problem is to meet the problem head-on, face-to-face. In the end I moved back Georgia.

# 8
# BLACK MAN

**Just a few** years ago, in 2006, my grandfather passed, but before he did I was taught so much. He owned a concrete construction company, a bar and lounge, land, and a few multifamily units. Needless to say, he died leaving his children and wife a solid foundation to build on. He raised his family in a small town across the water from Seattle, called Bremerton, Washington. He worked for the Puget Sound Shipyard for several years and retired from that job.

He started off with a family of thirteen, providing for them with the job at the shipyard. They lived on a piece of land that his parents gave him.

My grandfather told me a story about a gentleman who came to him in 1984 or 1985 and asked if he wanted to purchase shares of a company at twenty-five cents per share. He told the gentleman no. He told him no not because the man was untrustworthy but simply because he did not understand the way that stocks truly worked. Fast forward to over twenty years later; he told me during a dinner at a Chinese buffet in Silverdale that had he purchased the shares with $1,000 he would be a millionaire ten times over. He never regretted the decision; it was just a lesson learned. From that day on, he always kept $1,000 in his pocket to capitalize on any and every opportunity that might come his way. What I learned from this story is to always keep a certain amount of capital on hand or available to take advantage of opportunities. It doesn't have to be as much as $1,000, or it could be more, but whatever it is always be prepared for a capitalizing opportunity.

My grandfather did not trust banks; therefore he never had a bank account. He believed in safes, which is what I understand to be the only way that you can check your account balance, and no matter if we are in a recession or depression, the safe will still have my money that I deposited in it. My grandfather was born during the Great Depression, so it was evident where his ideals came from. During his childhood there were no jobs. In 1932 my grandfather was around five years old; unemployment was around 23 percent. By the time he was ten in 1937, unemployment was down to around 14 percent. In 1943 he started working at Puget Sound Shipyard during World War II, and the newly found economic boom began.

In my lifetime I've seen banks fail, and we may see it again. Even if we don't, we know for sure how the banks work; we know that banks are only required to keep a small percentage of their deposits. Therefore, they lend our savings out as they come in. This isn't really solid savings. What this lesson taught me was simply to find a safe place to stash your savings. A place where your cash will always be there, and there's no possibility of it not being there when you need it.

As I look at and reflect on my grandfather's life, he never went to college, he had thirteen children, and somehow he accumulated a small fortune. If we were to look at his financial picture, it would show four forms of income: first form from his shipyard retirement, second form from rent from his multifamily units, third form from his restaurant, The Hickory House, and fourth form from his concrete business. Without college my grandfather was able to put together a portfolio that could grow itself and expand itself, with, of course, a little management here and there.

The one thing that made my grandfather stand out was the fact that he paid cash for everything. Cash for properties, cars, and anything else you could imagine. I watched my own father pay for over twenty years on a house that was foreclosed on; if we do the math, the house was $90,000, and at $800 a month for twenty years, it equates to over $190,000. Before the downturn of the market, the phrase "Build wealth using other people's money" became very popular. But in reality you are building anything but wealth; you're building liability and debt until all properties are paid off completely and deeds and/or titles are held. I learned from my grandpa that if you purchase something with cash and you own it, no one can ever take it away. Whether the market is up or down, whether recession or depression, when you own it, you own it. This is what is called "true ownership."

# 9
# WHITE MAN (JIM)

**Arriving back in** the state of Georgia meant that this time things had to be different. I had to approach life more proactively because, for sure, it was time to pick up the pieces to my shattered life. First I had to get a job and begin working. Yes, I knew this, but admittedly I was a little lazy. I hadn't worked in almost a full year, which means I had gotten used to getting up when I wanted to, coming and going as I pleased, and so on. But that had to change because I didn't have any money to start my own business. So I had to get a job with benefits and retirement and this had to be my new launching pad. The only way to get such a thing meant I had to get up, go out, and physically avail myself. I began working for a company called QuikTrip Incorporated, and after working there for a while, I started to monitor the market again. I had somewhat of an idea how to follow and not get burned as severely this time. I felt as if I followed the money, I could see where the money trail would lead, and when I found that company or person, then and only then would I invest in that company or person's investments. I began doing my research to build myself into a stronger, more knowledgeable investor. The deeper I looked, the more depressing the news; I was also angered by what was going on with the market. The good thing was it made me realize that money could be made in the future because of what was going on now. Our economy is set on a boom/bust cycle. We had the boom, and the bubble had just burst. The greatest part of this was that the bubble was formulating again even though there was hardly air in it; it was formulating, and this became a reality. I couldn't get it out of my mind, which meant that I was now looking for an investment religiously—more specifically a stock or stocks that usually performed above average.

I began talking to any and everybody who looked like they had some knowledge about what I needed. I started with the individuals who came into QuikTrip early in the morning for their coffee before heading to work. I came upon people who worked for a southern company—Delta, Lab Corp, and other big companies that did well in market performance. As I talked to one customer I didn't know, I asked about their job's stock and an interesting conversation ensued. It just so happened that an older gentleman who stood behind him seemed to be intrigued by my conversation and asked if I had time when I got off work to talk. "Sure," I figured, why not?

The white gentleman and I met at McDonald's. He had arrived first, and as I entered a short time later, I noted his appearance and aura seemingly all at once. He sat stoic with two coffees in front of him. He had gray hair and crystal blue eyes. He was clean shaven, no facial hair at all. His shirt was pressed, his slacks were creased, and his fingers manicured. He had a gold diamond-studded ring on his right ring finger. The brilliance of the diamonds literally blinded me as they shimmered with the slightest motion of his hand. As I approached the table where he sat, I wondered why I was there. Curious, I took my seat.

He began our time together with a series of what I considered ice-breaker questions. Do you have kids? Do you live in a house? Are you in school? he asked. Then he began telling me about himself. He was from South Carolina. He'd moved to Chicago when he was a young adult to begin his life as a barber. Somewhere in there he learned a lot and created a great deal of wealth. He told me that Chicago was backward and crooked; everyone was crooked in one way or another, from police officers to politicians to anyone who held a position of authority. After briefly talking about himself, he got straight to the point: he said he wanted to teach me the only things I needed to know about the market if I really want to make money in it. I am definitely interested, I thought. This is exactly what I spent most of the last six years of my life trying to figure out. He said to look for these small details and you'll never go wrong. And, wow, was he right!

He began by explaining that every year there will be a moving sector of the market. First, find the moving sector, whether it's tech stocks, finance, real estate, or health. He was adamant about not allowing money to just sit and how important it was for money to constantly move. After finding the moving sector, look for the surge. A surge is when the price of a stock jumps upward more than 15 to 20 percent. After the surge wait for the 20 or more percent drawback. After or during the drawback, check to see what the insiders and financial institutions are doing. Are they buying or selling? Then check the volume; that means find out how many shares are being traded so when it's time to get out of a trade, the volume supports it.

The biggest, most important thing about my first conversation with Jim was that this was exactly what I was looking for. I could pick out good stocks, stable stocks, high-risk stocks with upward mobility. However, I still needed to learn when to buy shares and when to sell the shares. That is the single most important thing about trading the market. Everyone always says buy low and sell high, but they fail to say what to look for. All the questions I had searched through for answers in various financial books were answered solely and simply by Jim.

# 10
# AFGHAN (KEN)

**One Wednesday morning** around five o'clock, a gentlemen named Ken walked into QuikTrip and told me to keep an eye out for a particular guy who came in fairly regularly and tended to steal. No news to me since, in truth, this guy has stolen before. No sooner than I'd gotten the warning, the thief who Ken was speaking of walked up and asked me what Ken had just said. So there I was in an awkward position. I didn't want to lie to the customer, nor tell the truth for that matter. Nonetheless, I did what I felt was ethically correct and told him the truth. Extremely annoyed, the man turned and pushed his way outside to confront Ken. I don't know what words were exchanged, but I wasn't going outside to find out.

A few weeks passed after the incidence, and I was going about my days as usual. I was still the positive-energy, smiling, happy-go-lucky person I'd been, but Ken was still obviously angry and wouldn't talk to me at all. Not one word. He usually came in for coffee and would come to the counter to pay for it with a joke or two. But now he was coming straight in, grabbing his coffee, slamming the dollar on the counter, muttering to me to keep the change, and walking out the store. One day I asked Ken if he had forgiven me yet. He said, "No, you should not have told that guy our conversation." I explained to him what happened and how I did what I felt was ethically right. A few days after talking it out, Ken began to open back up little by little. One morning he came in with a smile and said, "We're going to have a positive day today." Puzzled, I asked, "What do you mean by 'we will have a positive day'?" "The market will be up," he answered. For the next weeks, he called it day after day, and he was right every single time. I didn't understand how he could be that good. He gave me a few stocks to look into: MU, Fifth Third Bank, and NCT.

I monitored these stocks periodically, and over a three-month period they increased dramatically, doubling and tripling in value. He definitely knew what he was doing. Day to day Ken would make thousands of dollars, and every other day he'd lose hundreds. He was what is called a "day trader." And he was really good at what he does.

Between the hours of 9:00 a.m. and 4:00 p.m. he

sat in front of two or three twenty-four-inch screens monitoring the market in real time, receiving real-time quotes and real-time news. But I still didn't understand how he called the market every day, so I asked him one morning and his reply was "Kevin, it's simple. You just have to look at the industrial averages. If the averages are positive, the market will be up. If the averages are negative, the market will be down. If there are two positives and one negative, the positives tend to pull the negative up, and if there are two negatives and one positive, the negatives will pull the positives down. It's just that simple." Yeah, to him it was simple, in fact, too simple to be true. However, as I monitored the market, it proved itself to be true day in and day out. This had been the missing key to my whole understanding.

What I learned from these three men, from three different walks of life and three totally different backgrounds, connected a small portion of the entire market. First Jim taught me when to buy and sell and to know that sometimes there will be drastic changes in the market; for instance some days the market will drop several points. Now back when I didn't know that, I wouldn't know to pull out of a stock before the drop, so that information was valuable but it wasn't enough to sustain a positive investment return with the Forex or the stock market. When Ken walked into my life and gave me information that helped me know when to buy and when to sell currency, that connected the Forex and the stock market together, so I would be able to make profiting trades from day to day. The only problem was trying to figure out whether the day was going to be up or down so I would know whether to buy or sell for that day. Ken put the last puzzle piece into perspective.

What I learned from these three men has pointed me into the direction of success and financial freedom. These three individuals who know absolutely nothing about each other changed my life for the better without knowing about each other. As far as I was concerned, I could now be the financially independent man that I'd wanted to be since getting out of the military. Using the lessons I learned from the black man, the white man, and the Afghan, I put a strategy together. People say they want to show you how to make money, or they say, "Do what I do and you'll make money." No one ever showed me exactly how, and no one ever showed me the important parts that actually make the money. Like a boasting peacock, they always showed the aftereffects of the money but never each step taken, the rules behind each step, or why they took the particular steps in the particular order they did. But in this little book, I'm going to show you exactly how by first doing a recap of the lessons learned from the black man, white man, and Afghan.

Find the moving sector of the market:
- Look at its fifty-two-week highs and lows. (Try to

purchase the stock closer to its fifty-two-week. for long-term trades.)

- After the surge wait for a 15 to 20 percent drawback before buying. (This is true for stocks and currency.)
- Check the volume. Look for at least a 50 percent or more increase in volume.
- Before pulling the trigger, check and see what the insiders and big institutional holders are doing. (This is only true for stocks.)
- Check to see whether the market will be up or down by looking at the industrial averages at the beginning of the trading day. (This is true for currency and stocks.)
- If the market is up, the dollar will be weak, so buy the US dollar from the other currency pair, just so that we are on the same page, a currency pair is the value of once currency against another. For example the value of the United Stated Dollar (USD) compared to the Japenese Yen (JPY), the currency pair would be displayed as USD/JPY
- If the market is down, the dollar is strong, so sell the US dollar to the other currency pair.

With the rules and regulations set forth this is what needs to take place:

Open a Forex trading account with no less than one hundred dollars. Do it in a foreign account with a foreign brokerage if possible because US brokers only allow traders to trade up; when trading with US brokers, a trader can only profit from buy trades when the currency is trading up and cannot profit from sell trades when the currency is trading down. Foreign brokers allow you to profit from buy and sell trades. Also it would be great to open a stock brokerage account with the minimum, which for some brokerages is $500, but it may range up to $2,000 or more.

When you start trading currency, look for the sector that is moving. Find as many stocks as possible in that sector and begin monitoring them—five to three is a decent amount. Check their fifty-two-week highs and lows. See who the insiders are and what big institutional holders are invested in them. Make sure the insiders and institutions aren't ditching the stock or selling off their shares. Follow the stock, wait for the surge, and if there's no surge but it's trending up, wait for the pullback. The drop has to be at least 15 to 20 percent, and then buy. Watch the stock every day, week after week, month after month. Wait for the profit to come along. One thing that's very important about profit is your exit strategy. The entry strategy is very precise and clear, but just as important as the entry strategy is the exit strategy; it has equal importance. Please remember that. I cannot give you a precise one, two, three on the exit strategy because it varies. My personal exit strategy is at least 100 percent profit or 10 percent loss with currency, and 25 percent profit and 8 percent loss with stocks. This means if I invest in a stock or currency and my position made 100 percent or 25 percent profit, I get out of the trade, unless I was getting into the trade to hold a long-term position. If, after getting into a trade, I lose 10 to 8 percent, I pull out of the trade with a loss. This may sound too good to be true, so I tell you what. Do a mock test, and make the trades with fake money to see how well it works.

# 11
# RESTRUCTURE

**A beast was** born December 22, 1983, in a small town called Bremerton, Washington, and his name was Kevin Cody. I became a free man at the age of twenty-two when I learned one of the greatest lessons known to man, and that is: the only person or thing that can stop me from doing whatever I wish in life is solely me, no one else. I choose whether I fail or I succeed, and for sure I choose to succeed. However, the first few years of my young adult life and the last few years of my young adult life I chose to fail, but now it's 2010 and I'm deciding to succeed. I'm going as far as I want to go and taking whomever feels the same way with me. I have the know-how, the self-control, and the discipline it takes to do so.

The struggling will stop now. The thing about finances is nobody wants to talk about them. Why?

Because they're personal. They're as sacred as marriage. There are a few nonprofit organizations created to help people get out of debt. But I've found a lot of the agencies to be nowhere near helpful at all. Instead they are actually harmful. They are supposed to help people who are in debt get out of debt, relieve stress, and get their lives back on track, but they cause more stress than they relieve. What most financial advisers and professional money managers will do is simply tell you how much debt you are in, how much it will take monthly to get out of that debt, and the amount of years it will take to pay it off. The problem is the amount of years is forever! Most of the time, when someone is in debt, it is because of his or her spending habits. Think about it: if we weren't paying our debtors in the first place and our debts were a hundred dollars a month here and seventy-nine dollars a month there, realistically, are we going to pay $779 a month to pay them all? This can be emotionally stressful.

When it comes to our emotions, we need to know how to take full control. We first have to control our thinking and really begin training ourselves to think about the differences between wants and needs. Even if we were to consolidate all of our debts and bring our monthly debt payments from $779 to $279, that extra $500 will be just right to party with, buy clothes, and take care of other wants. This money doesn't even have to be for investing. This is the key to getting out of debt.

There are many things people want in life. Most of the things wanted or needed require capital. I have the number to make that possible. That number is $500,000. Some people feel they need millions. But as I explain, you will see exactly why that number is sufficient. Let me break this down.

First you have to understand monthly expenses and debts. My definition of monthly expenses is expenses that you pay on a monthly basis for services used. My definition of debts is money borrowed for anything. That being said, I have come to the conclusion that a house is not an asset; in my opinion it is debt. The only way your house is an asset is when you own it completely and have only to pay taxes and insurance on it; then and only then is it an asset. Cars are a debt or liability if you have a car note. If you no longer owe the bank for your car and you have the title, then and only then is your car an asset. Utilities are a monthly expense; services are used, therefore services are paid for. Other monthly expenses would include cell phone and water bills. So back to the magic number: $500,000 will allow me to live the rest of my life comfortably. I will be able to make a modest $24,000 a year and have a little over $1,200 a month to do whatever I want to do. I will have the option to double my income if I choose to work anywhere. But first things first. I have to pay off all of my debts and maintain a zero balance on all debts. No loans whatsoever. In conversations with Jim, he always made the point that cash is king— no car loans, no school loans, no mortgages, no credit cards, etc. Don't borrow any money from anyone. After paying off my debts, I must begin saving and investing. The saving and investing split is sixty-forty. Of the funds set aside for saving and investing purposes, 60 percent of it will be invested and the other 40 percent will be saved until reaching safe, modest savings numbers. Most financial advisers encourage their clients to have three to six months of their monthly income saved. Once this amount is reached, add to that a $2,500 to $5,000 emergency fund account.

During the brief moment in life when I was debt free, it felt great to owe no one anything, especially since at one point I felt that I ownmy life. I had complete control over my life, but as long as I was in debt, I was in fact enslaved, not in a black-white fashion but to the wealthy. Yes, I was enslaved to them. We always hear people talk about "them," the wealthy. "They're trying to stop me..." "They ain't trying to pay nobody..." "They ain't trying to help nobody but themselves..."

Listen, people aren't talking or complaining about a race of people; they are talking or complaining about a class of people. Wealth has no face or race.

Let me take a moment to explain the difference between wealthy and rich. Grandpa, Jim, and Ken are wealthy; they don't have tens of millions of dollars, but they have enough to where none of them have to work. They all reached their magic numbers. They don't have to work another day in their lives, and their money will still flow. They can live as if they're on permanent paid vacation.

However, everyone's number is different; it depends on his or her wants and needs. Wealth is the ability to make enough income to sustain your lifestyle whether your j-o-b continues or not. Rich is when a lot of money is made from working; the unfortunate thing about that is that once the work stops, the money stops, and everything connected to it comes to a halt. In other words wealthy individuals make $100,000 a year when they're working and when they're not. Rich individuals make $100,000 a year when they're working, and zero when they're not. I want you to know the difference and live the life you want.

## 50/30/20

This rule came from my three mentors—the black man, the white man, and the afghan. Taking everything that I've learned from these extraordinary men and applying it to my personal financial life will create increasing results year after year It will create increasing results year after year. The idea behind the rule is that as your income grows, your wealth grows, and as your wealth grows, your income grows. It's a revolving cycle that feeds itself. So instead of running on a treadmill as fast as you can, staying in one spot, it will be more like running up an endless mountain with the top nowhere in sight.

The 50/30/20 rule is applied when 50 percent of income is saved and invested, 30 percent of income is spent on needs/necessities such as rent, mortgage, food, water, sewage, garbage, taxes, insurance, electricity, and gas. Twenty percent of income is spent on luxuries such as Internet, cell phones, gym memberships, and pretty much anything else that is a want. Let's remember, what I believe to be needs, others don't; so we could define needs as essential items or services used to sustain life. No, cell phones don't sustain life, and although a Benz may feel nice to drive, it does not sustain life. Utilizing this rule allows you to actually build wealth faster and easier. When you think about the idea of the 50/30/20 rule, it seems like it's barely enough to get by. But let's break it down.

The average single person with no kids, making on average $2,000 a month, can actually apply this rule and have a great life without penny-pinching. After taxes, this person would have a little over $800 for necessities and luxury items and would have put away $800. At the end of one year, this person would have $9,600 saved and invested. Depending on the investment choices, even a little more because of gains and dividends paid out throughout the year. This would be a wealthy example of the 50/30/20 rule.

Most of us live over our means or, to be as blunt as possible, spend more than what we have. For the average person making $2,000, the monthly expense report may have 120 percent of his or her income going toward necessities and luxury items—for instance, $800 a month for rent alone simply because they feel that it is affordable since they make a little less than three times the amount of rent, and another $300 to $500 going toward food, water, and electricity. But for most of this general category, which I lived in myself for half of my young adult years, the other half of this income goes straight to vehicles. When I say that a car can cost upwards of $700 per month, most people don't believe me. A home and a car shouldn't cost the same every month. So let's look at it. The average car note is $300 a month or more, gas is on average three dollars per gallon, and the average tank holds fifteen gallons; therefore, to fill the tank costs on average forty-five dollars a week, which is about $180 per month. Car insurance is on average $180 per month; if the car is owned flat out, depending on how much coverage you have, we could break that number in half. In addition, we have to hope that the price of fuel doesn't go up to four dollars and change like it normally does throughout the year, and that work and home are our only destinations, which is also not the case. Therefore, these numbers were lowballed for the benefit of the reader.

Some people are just about there but not quite. Most people who look at their 401K and believe they can just sit back and continue to let 3 percent before taxes come out of their checks on a monthly basis are setting themselves up for failure. Yes, compounded interest and dividend payments will pay off in the long run, but the rate of inflation, I believe, is a little more than 3 percent, so technically you're flatlining. The average person making $2,000 a month would only be putting away sixty dollars a month, about $720 for the whole year. The rest of his or her income after taxes is spent. This person is not living above his or her means; this person is spending exactly what he or she makes, nothing over. This is usually the category of check-to-check workers.

This is a rule strictly to build wealth. Most financial books tell you how to cut costs and how to budget but never how to divide your income for a specific goal; this one does. There's no such thing as getting rich quick, but if there was a fast way to build wealth, this would be the fastest. Notice I didn't say easy, simply because if you're human, your emotions will get the best of you when deciding what costs to cut to get ahead. It is easy to think about but not necessarily easy to do.

The most important reason why anyone should use this rule of thumb is to establish wealth, no matter how small the amount. There is one fact about using this rule: it will always put the individual in a position to take advantage of the economic downturns, no matter how deep or slight. Because, of course, the seasoned investor knows to always buy when everyone else is selling. When you think about it, the amount of funds that are saved in low-risk investments are available for you to place in the market when it is down whether it be stocks, commodities, or the real estate market. You will always be ready.

This is how you know it will really help. Let's think for a second about our income, and let's think at the end of each year how much money we've actually saved. Most of the time it's not even 10 percent; in fact we may have saved less than what we paid in taxes for that year, if we saved anything. If I am always putting away 50 percent of my income, then no matter how much money I make—whether it be $1,000 per month, $5,000 per month, or $10,000 per month—my wealth will continuously grow. My liquid assets will grow at least half of whatever my income is on a yearly basis. If I lose my job's $10,000 per month salary, and my salary decreases to $5,000 per month, I will still have $60,000 or more of liquid assets.

In reality most of us really do live check to check. So the idea of living on 50 percent of our income is really unrealistic. The truth is it all depends on how far you, the individual or the couple, is willing to step back. The further the step back, the faster you will begin to accumulate and build wealth. For example, the average couple has a house and a few cars and a few cell phones. Maybe even the children have cell phones. The average couple lives in a decent-sized house with a mortgage payment, taxes, and insurance that take up half of their income. The thought or idea of moving out of this beautiful house, or selling the Benz or BMW, is really out of the question. One step back is just cutting off luxuries like cell phones, Internet, and cable. Two steps back would be selling the cars or possibly giving one or both cars back. Three steps back would be getting rid of everything as if you didn't make a dime. So when looking at this analogy, if I took one step back, I could take a small leap forward, two steps back could give me a bit more of a start, but three steps back would give me a running start. Each step is cutting costs until your costs are essentially obsolete. All the income that will be virtually profit to began stashing. It's not easy, but it is what I like to call "the battle of emotions."

Now that we understand that first half of the 50/30/20 rule, we can break down the 50 percent of income that is supposed to be saved and invested. We break down the 50% into another 50/30/20. The fifty is to save and invest in a CD, MMA, or money market accounts, saving bonds, or savings account; these are all low-risk investments that don't yield much but have the lowest risk of all investments. The thirty will be invested in medium-risk investments, such as mutual funds or blue cap companies such as Walmart and/or Coca-Cola. And twenty will be invested in high-risk investments such as penny stocks, which are viewed in many cases as stocks under five dollars, as well as Forex, which is an exchange for trading foreign currency from other countries. Of course the higher the risk, the bigger the return. So we don't need much to make big returns. For example, $600 in CTIC at the beginning of 2009 was only six cents a share. This would have bought you ten thousand shares. By the middle of the year, it was $1.20 a share, and toward the end of the year around twelve dollars. Yes, this would have turned your $600 into $120,000. But this stock was also considered to be a high risk. Although this stock would have created a nice gain, ten others just like it would have gone bankrupt, such as Charter, which was around the same time four cents per share. Charter restructured, and although it filed for bankruptcy, it did a reverse split, and now it looks like a healthy company. A reverse split is when a company gives you a lesser amount of shares per share that you own. For example, $400 would have bought you ten thousand shares of CHTR at the time. If Charter did a 10,000:1 split, that would mean for every ten thousand shares you owned, you would receive one share; if it's the other way around, a 1:10,000 split, that means for every one share, you would receive 10,000 shares; this a regular\stock split.

As you can see, low risk gives less reward, and high risk gives more reward. Although every high-risk investment may not give you the return that you're looking for, when the high risk does give you a return, it will give you a nice high return and, nine times out of ten, will beat whatever gains you made from all of your investments that year.

# 12

# THE MOVEMENT

**I believe there** are three types of people: there are people who make problems, people who point out problems, and people who solve problems. It's easy to make problems, and it's also easy to point out problems. The most challenging is solving the problem. This is my idea of an attempt to solve the financial problems of future generations. This movement is an attempt to challenge the minds of our youth and prepare them with the knowledge of finance before moving forward in life, starting at eleventh grade because at this point we may have our first job or business, whether it's babysitting or cutting lawns. If we plant a financial seed in a generation's mind, we can change the course of our generation's wealth. The movement will also help parents of the youth become great examples of what to do and what not to do with finances.

For example, a lot of our parents went to college and have college debts, got their jobs and are making good money. Our parents bought a house or maybe two, and now they have mortgages. On top of all of this, they now have nice bold cars, and with the cars are most likely car notes. Therefore our parents show us the lifestyle of the past, the life of going to work to pay bills, and not necessarily a financial-free life. How often were our parents able to go on vacation, and if they did what was life like for a few months after the vacation? Sometimes the vacation was even placed on a credit card. The fact is our parents lived by the old rules of life; we must change those rules to rules that will allow us to grow financially.

The reason for starting the movement is because it seems as if, when I was around eighteen, there was no one to really guide me financially. I believe that we should surround ourselves with like-minded people. So if you're into music, you surround yourself with musicians; if you're religious, you surround yourself with religious people. And if you are broke and want to be wealthy and change life for you and the generations behind you, surround yourself with those types of people. This movement will surround me with like-minded individuals just like me who have the drive and determination to change the outlook of their financial wealth.

The movement will utilize the 50/30/20 rule to its max capacity, showing in real time the step-by-step moves that will increase the wealth of its members slowly but surely and steadily. The movement should give each member insight on the inner workings of various investments from the purchasing of real estate properties to renting out those properties, from purchasing stock to purchasing tax lien, and from trading currency to buying into businesses. The movement will do all of these things in real time. There will be failures as well as successes in all the investments that the movement includes itself in.

You may have had heard the phrases "If I only…," "I wish I had…," and "Man, I missed out on an opportunity of a lifetime." This will be you. The movement will not be a get-rich-quick scheme or a multilevel network marketing business. It will be a private, silent investment club, teaching its members what to do with leftover funds, and showing the beginning steps and the process of investments as well as the result of the investments made. It will give each member opportunities to do more than just watch from the sidelines and also invest in the project personally. Either way all members will get exposure and opportunity to gain. For example, each member will get a percentage of the profit split, regardless of if they invested personal initial investments or not. Simply by being a member, if a project makes a profit, a portion of the profits will be distributed to members. Direct investors, those who choose to invest directly in a project, will get their equal share of the profit.

## Sample Breakdown
### Project XYZ

| | |
|---|---|
| Initial investment | $10,000 |
| R2R2W 10% | $1,000 |
| Direct Investor A 45% | $4,500 |
| Direct Investor B 45% | $4,500 |
| Total | $10,000 |
| Project XYZ gross | $50,000 |
| Less initial investment | $10,000 |
| Net Profit | $40,000 |
| R2R2W 10% | $4,000 |
| Direct Investor 45% | $18,000 |
| Direct Investor 45% | $18,000 |
| Total | $40,000 |

Most people will not invest in anything because either they don't understand the nature of the investment or don't want to take the risk. This statement applies to almost everyone. From conversations I've had with people of various backgrounds, the point that each person will make is "I work hard for my money, I don't want to lose it, and I definitely don't want to put it into anything that has the possibility of failing" At that point in the conversation, typically I leave the subject matter alone. But now I make the following point for anyone with that same philosophy or ideal: your job is a company, and someone took a chance to start that company. As an employee for that company, you are taking a chance on that company in the following ways: One, if the job does not make a profit, the job will fire you; you will be jobless and go through a period of time when you will be looking for another chance to take on another company. Two, depending on one source of income or one opportunity to finance your life is leaving more opportunity for failure. For those individuals afraid to take a chance on an opportunity or investment, the movement is for you.

This movement will educate its members by showing live and interactive investments designed so members will see the investment perform from the planning phase to the execution phase to the reaping-the-rewards phase. They will see this over and over again with all types of investment projects from stocks to bonds and from real estate purchases to business start-ups.

The goal of the movement is to encourage and enlighten members to begin investing in themselves and their futures.

CPSIA information can be obtained at www.ICGtesting.com
Printed in the USA
LVOW13s0158200314

378039LV00001BA/5/P